Big Book of BUDS

of

GREATEST HITS

W9-CWA-235

Marijuana Varieties from the World's Best Breeders

Ed Rosenthal

Quick American Publishing

Big Book of Buds Greatest Hits — Marijuana Varieties from the World's Best Breeders (Vol. 5)
Copyright © 2016 Ed Rosenthal
Published by Quick American Publishing
A Division of Quick Trading Co.
Piedmont, CA, USA

Printed in China
FIRST PRINTING

ISBN: 978-1-936807-32-1
eISBN: 978-1-936807-33-8
Executive Editor: Ed Rosenthal
Project Director: Jane Klein
Project Manager: Darcy Thompson
Chief Editor: Ellen Holland
Editorial Assistance: Sidney Borghino
Photo Editors: Darcy Thompson, Christian Petke
Design: Scott Idleman / Blink

Variety and breeder stories have previously appeared in The Big Book of Buds Volumes 1-4

Photographs of varieties appear courtesy of the seed companies. All other photos by Ed Rosenthal unless
otherwise credited.
Cover Photo: The Church, Green House Seed Co.

Library of Congress Control Number: 2016938142

This book is dedicated to Nikolai Vavilov 1887-1943

Nikolai Vavilov was a prominent Russian botanist and geneticist who developed the theory of the centers of origin of cultivated plants. He studied and improved cereal crops and had a keen interest in cannabis. He created seed banks still in existence to preserve valuable landraces. Nikolai was executed by the Soviets because his science was in conflict with their ideology.

Acknowledgements

K. Abellán, Sidney Borghino, Ani Chamichian, C.R.A.F.T. Collective, William Dolphin, Marc Emery, Ellen Holland, Bonnie King, Jane Klein, Shelli Newhart, PhD, Christian Petke, Pistils, DJ Short, Jason Schulz, Darcy Thompson, Chris X, PhD

There are things you can replace
And others you cannot
The time has come to weigh those things
This space is gettin' hot

Lyrics from song "Althea"
Words by Robert Hunter; Music by Jerry Garcia
Reproduced by arrangement with Ice Nine Publishing

Photo: Jack the Ripper - TGA Genetics, Subcool Seeds

Contents

Seed Companies & Varieties

Barney's Farm
Barney's Farm Blue cheese
Dr. Grinspoon
Barney's Farm GI3 Haze
LSD
Morning Glory
Vanilla Kush

BC Bud Depot
BC Blueberry
BC God Bud
BC Sweet Tooth
The Purps

Big Buddha Seeds
Big Buddha Cheese
Blue Cheese
Bubble Cheese
Buddha Haze
Cheesus
Chiesel
G Bomb
The Kali

Ceres Seeds
Easy Rider
Fruity Thai
Skunk Haze
White Smurf

Delta 9 Labs
Fruit of the Gods

DJ Short
Blueberry
Flo
Grape Kush

DNA Genetics
Headband (Reserva Privada)
LA Confidential
Lemon Skunk

Dr. Atomic
Atomic Northern Lights

Dr. Greenthumb Seeds
Iranian Autoflower

Dutch Passion
Mazar
Orange Bud
Power Plant
Strawberry Cough
The Ultimate

Flying Dutchman
Afghanica
Arctic Sun
Aurora B.
Dutchmen's Royal Orange
Pineapple Punch
The Pure Skunk #I

Green House Seed Co.
Big Bang
Hawaiian Snow
Nevil's Haze
White Widow
White Rhino
Strawberry Haze (Arjan's)
Super Lemon Haze
Super Silver Haze
The Church
The Doctor

High Bred Seeds
Lowryder #2

KC Brains
Leda Uno
Mango

Magus Genetics
Double Dutch
Motavation

Mandala Seeds
Hashberry
Kalichakra
White Satin

Master Thai Organics
Tahoe Gold

Mr. Nice Seed Bank
Medicine Man

Nirvana Seed Bank
Ice
Master Kush
NYPD

Paradise Seeds
Jacky White
Nebula
Wappa
White Berry

Sagarmatha
Matanuska Tundra

Sannies Seeds
Jack F6

Sensi Seed Bank
American Dream
Big Bud
Black Domina
California Indica
Ed Rosenthal Super Bud
First Lady
Hash Plant
Jack Herer
Northern Lights
Northern Lights-Haze

Serious Seeds
AK 47
Chronic
Kali Mist
White Russian

Soma's Sacred Seeds
Amnesia Haze
New York City Diesel

TGAgenetics Subcool Seeds
Jack the Ripper
Jilly Bean
Querkle
Vortex

TH Seeds
A-Train
Kushage
Sage

Varieties by Indica & Sativa Classification

Varieties by Indica, Sativa and Ruderalis

 Indica Strains (90% to 100%)

Barney's Farm Blue cheese
Big Buddha Cheese
Black Domina
California Indica
Dutchmen's Royal Orange
First Lady
G-Bomb
Hash Plant
Iranian Autoflower
LA Confidential
Mango
Northern Lights
Vanilla Kush
Wappa

 Indica Dominant Strains (60% to 90%)

Atomic Northern Lights
BC Blueberry
BC God Bud
BC Sweet Tooth
Big Bang
Big Bud
Blueberry
Blue Cheese

Bubble Cheese
Cheesus
Double Dutch
Easy rider
Ed Rosenthal Super Bud
Grape Kush
Hashberry
Headband
Jilly Bean
Lowryder #2
LSD
Master Kush
Matanuska Tundra
Mazar
Querkle
Tahoe Gold
The Church
The Doctor
The Kali
The Ultimate
White Berry
White Rhino

 Sativa Strains (90 to 100%)

Dr. Grinspoon
Jack F6
Kali Mist

Sativa Dominant (60 to 90%)

A-Train

AK 47

Amnesia Haze

Arctic Sun

Aurora B.

Barney's Farm Gl3 Haze

Buddha Haze

Chiesel

Chronic

Flo

Fruit of the Gods

Fruity Thai

G-BombFirst Lady

Hawaiian Snow

Ice

Jack Herer

Jack the Ripper

Jacky White

Kalichakra

Kushage

Leda Uno

Lemon Skunk

Medicine Man

Motavation

Nebula

Nevil's Haze

New York City Diesel

Northern Lights-Haze

NYPD

Orange Bud

Pineapple Punch

Power Plant

Sage

Skunk Haze

Strawberry Cough

Strawberry Haze (Arjan's)

Super Lemon Haze

Super Silver Haze

The Pure Skunk #I

The Purps

White Russian

White Satin

White Smurf

White Widow

 ## Ruderalis and Ruderalis Hybrids

Easy Rider

 ## Autoflower

Easy Rider

Lowryder #2

Introduction

Introduction

By Ed Rosenthal

Humans and marijuana have been in a long-term love affair that probably began in the Stone Age when someone harvested the dried leaves to stoke a fire. Since that auspicious occurrence, the two species have had a special relationship that has lasted 3,000 generations — likely longer than with any other plant — but for as long as this tie has endured, its viability has been tested.

Until college — before the drug war and during the folk music era, where I hung out with other discontents stoking the embers of the drug and alcohol scarred Beat Generation — I had never encountered weed. Then, during my second experience, I realized that this herb was my ally, helping me to overcome emotional crises.

Marijuana has continued to help me throughout my life. It has made me a better, happier, more caring person and assisted me in getting past the set perceptions that I was taught or learned through society's implicit instruction book. It guides me to think outside the box and spurs creativity. And I know I'm not the only one.

I discovered marijuana just as society was re-discovering it. During the 19th and early 20th centuries and for thousands of years before it was well known as a medicine and for its recreational value. In the early 20th century government pol-icy lead to its demonization, then to its criminal-ization and finally to its cultural genocide as society forgot about cannabis leading to almost total ignorance of the plant and its many qualities.

The lasting symbiotic relationship we have had with this plant exists because cannabis is a rogue, a tramp and a helper. Its relationship to humans is so profound that there is no such thing as wild cannabis, only feral populations escaped from domestication. That's what makes it rogue. Unlike many domesticated plants, including grains, it can live without human intervention, as it waits to be rediscovered by a new generation willing to experiment with it.

Marijuana and hemp have repeatedly helped humans to take a jump to the next level, both materially and spiritually, and their story shows both the resilience and fragility of culture. If marijuana had not been rediscovered by the '60s and '70s experimental culture, the source of it all, the seeds — that is, the seeds from the landraces — might have been eradicated by international prohibitionists. In the U.S. the varieties grown for hemp throughout the 19th and mid-20th century have been lost. The seeds were destroyed or died the unnatural death of not being replanted and renewed.

If it weren't for the work of a few dedicated pioneers such as Robert Randall and Jack Herer we might never have known the benefits or true history of the plant. The thousands of years of human culture, plant breeding, knowledge and this valuable gift of nature would have been lost.

Cannabis provided its cultivators with an advantage that breeders of other annual plants do not have. It is dioecious, the plants are either male or female. So it's easy to separate the sexes and create seed. Other annuals carry both sexes on the same plant, making it harder to control pollination.

At first there were no seed companies, but early cultivators could easily produce their-own and then naturally, start breeding. This is still going on. Growers often breed their best plants. Outdoors, local varieties acclimated to the area are often traded among growers. The early pioneers worked mostly with seeds found in weed coming from the world over. Mostly from Mexico and Colombia but also Southeast Asia, the Hindu-Kush Hippie Trail and a trickle from Africa.

The first breeding wave saw selections of adapted landraces and hybrids modified to ripen outdoors or to be grown indoors. During this period "90-day wonders," suitable for growing indoors were considered cutting edge. These include Af-ghani and other Indicas often crossed with South African (Durban Poison), Mexican or Thai.

The second breeding wave resulted in the first complex hybrids. Breeders worked towards three goals: increasing potency, expanding yield and decreasing time to ripening.

As the Drug War and federal eradication program CAMP raged outdoors, indoor cultivation became more popular. For the first time, the major breeding emphasis was devoted to indoor crops. Domesticated strains were crossed with each other, and new imports from Africa, Brazil and India were introduced. Many of the strains introduced during this period are considered classics and are still popular and used in breeding programs. Strains developed during this period include Skunk #1, White Widow, Silver Haze and the notorious NL5-Haze.

The Third Wave began after the breeders adapted growing habits, made the plants more productive and raised potency. They then took an increased interest in flavors, tastes and aromas, which connoisseurs implicitly understood was closely associated with the high or medical effects. This represented the beginning of attempts by breeders to target specific effects. Some of the most popular varieties are the Diesel family, Jack the Ripper, and Cheeses.

After 40 years of growing and breeding marijuana we are now within the fifth decade and fourth generation of breeders. These breeders rarely start with the progenitor varieties seen in the earlier waves, relying instead on new sets of breeding stock such as modified Hazes, Headband and Blue Dream, to use as building blocks, occasionally adding early classics or landraces to the mix. This era too is coming to an end.

This book is a celebration of the work of marijuana breeders over the last 3,000 years. Like the corn, potatoes, wheat or tomatoes we eat, we now experience the efforts of only the last generations, those who built on the work of untold, unknown generations to bring us this precious, even sacred, produce. Here the knowledge of these generations is distilled in the varieties described, each also distilled from a single seed so tiny.

Prospects for the future look even more exciting. The next group of breeders includes people trained in breeding and genetics using science to guide them towards their goals; twisting the cannabis genome to enhance targeted characteristics. Get ready to jump from the next step to the unimaginable. Let's take flight.

Quick Key to Icons

English • En Español • Deutsch
En Français • Italiano • Nederlands

Strain Type

Sativa

Indica

Indica/Sativa

Sativa/Indica

Sativa/Ruderalis

Indica/Ruderalis

Sativa/Indica/Ruderalis

Feminized

Autoflower

Growing Info

Flowering Time
Tiempo de floración
Blütezeit
Durée de floraison
Stagione della fioritura
Bloetijd

Parentage
Genética
Mutterpflanze
Descendance
Genitori
Stamboom

Yield
Rendimiento
Ertag
Rendement
Raccolta
Opbrengst

Sea of Green

Screen of Green

Indoor
Interior
Drinnen
D'Intérieur
Dentro
Binnen

Outdoor
Exterior
Draussen
d'Extérieur
Fuori
Buiten

Indoor/Outdoor
Interior/Exterior
Drinnen/Draussen
d'Intérieur/d'Extérieur
Dentro/Fuori
Binnen/Buiten

Sensory Experience

Buzz
Efecto
die Art des Turns
Effets
Effetti
High Effekt

Taste/Smell
Sabor/Aroma
Geschmack/Geruch
Saveur/Arôme
Sapore/Odore
Smaak/Geua

Breeder Location

Canada

Netherlands

Spain

United Kingdom

U.S.A.

Switzerland

The Icons

The first icon deals with plant type. The possibilities are:

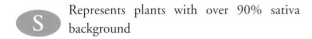 Represents plants with over 90% sativa background

Represents plants with over 90% indica background

Hybrids which are:

More sativa

More indica

Sativa plants grow from the equator through the 50th parallel. They include both marijuana and hemp varieties. The plants that interest marijuana growers come from the equator to the 20th parallel. Countries from this area are noted for high-grade marijuana and include Colombia, Jamaica, Nigeria, Congo, Thailand and Sumatra. Populations of plants from most of these areas are quite uniform for several reasons. Cannabis is not native to these areas. It was imported to grow hemp crops and then it adapted over many generations with human intervention. Each population originated from a small amount of fairly uniform seed from the 45–50th parallel. Then the populations evolved over hundreds of generations with the help of humans. This led to fairly uniform populations in climates that varied little year to year.

Sativas grow into 5–15 feet (1.5–4.5 meters) tall

symmetrical pine-shaped plants. The spaces between the leaves on the stem, the internodes, are longer on sativas than indicas. This helps to give sativas a taller stature. The lowest branches are the widest, spreading 1½ to 3 feet (.5–1 meter); since the branches grow opposite each other, plant diameter may reach 6 feet (1.8 meters). The leaves are long, slender, and finger-like. The plants are light green since they contain less chlorophyll.

Sativa buds are lighter than indicas. Some varieties grow buds along the entire branch, developing a thin but dense cola. Others grow large formations of more loose, spongy buds. The smoke is sweet and spicy or fruity. The highs are described as soaring, psychedelic, thoughtful, and spacy.

Indica plants originated around the 30th parallel in the Hindu Kush region of the Himalayan foothills. This includes the countries of Afghanistan, Pakistan, Tajikistan, Northern India, and Nepal. The weather there is quite variable from year to year. For this reason the populations in these regions have a varied gene pool. Even within a particular population there is a high degree of heterogeneity, which results in plants of the same variety having quite a bit of variability. This helps the population survive. No matter what the weather during a particular year, some plants will thrive and reproduce.

These plants are fairly short, usually under 5 feet (1.5 meters) tall. They are bushy with compact branching and short internodes. They range in shape from a rounded bush to a pine-like shape with a wide base. The leaves are short, very wide, and dark green when compared to most equatorial sativas because they contain larger amounts of chlorophyll. Sometimes there is webbing between the leaflets. At the 30th latitude, the plants don't receive as much light as plants at or near the equator. By increasing the amount of chlorophyll, the cells use light more efficiently.

Indica buds are dense and tight. They form several shapes depending on variety. All of them are chunky or blocky. Sometimes they form continuous clusters along the stem. They have intense smells ranging from acrid, skunky, or musky to deep pungent aromas reminiscent of chocolate, coffee, earth, or hash. Indica smoke is dense, lung expanding, and cough inducing. The high is heavy, body-oriented, and lethargic.

IS Indica-sativa hybrids naturally tend towards the indica side of the family. They usually have controlled height. They don't grow very tall and after forcing flowering, their growth is limited. Their side branching is usually not prominent and they can be grown in a small space. However, since they have both sativa and indica influences, they may include surprising hints of sativa in some aspect of the plant's makeup, the flavors, or the high.

SI Sativa-indica hybrids tend towards the sativa parentage. They are taller plants, which will grow to double or triple their size if they are forced when they are small. They are usually hard to grow in a sea of green, as the plants demand more space to spread out. However, the indica genetics may influence the size of the plant or its buds, the speed of flowering, the density of buds, the flavors, or the high.

SR A sativa-dominant variety crossed with auto-flowering ruderalis

IR An indica-dominant variety crossed with autoflowering ruderalis

SIR A combination of sativa, indica, and ruderalis genetics

R Ruderalis hybrids: In recent years, it has become more common to hear of the ruderalis variant of cannabis alongside indica and sativa. First encountered in Russia, ruderalis was named in 1924 and was often referred to as "weedy" cannabis because it was low in THC content and high in cannabidiol (CBD). Ruderalis plants are found in the wild in the far northern portions of the Caucuses Mountains and areas north of the 40th parallel in western Asia. Even though its smoke is nothing to brag about, ruderalis has one unique quality that has saved it from the trash bin of history. Unlike other forms of cannabis that require changes to the light cycle in order to begin flowering, ruderalis flowers automatically. More and more breeding projects are working with this cannabis subspecies to create autoflowering varieties.

The pure ruderalis is a short plant. It does not typically exceed a height of 1.5 feet (50 cm). It often grows as a single-stem plant, forming wide leaves and pinecone sized colas. Because of its size, ruderalis is sometimes called "bonsai" cannabis. Its smaller size also means it matures much more rapidly than most indicas and sativas. This was probably an adaptation to the short grow season of the Russian steppes. While pure ruderalis varieties do not possess enough desirable qualities to be commercially viable, ruderalis crosses abound right now in the marketplace. Most plants will have a more rapid season and form a shorter plant when crossed with ruderalis. In addition, ruderalis becomes synonymous with autoflowering varieties.

Because of their short growing season, these varieties have adapted by beginning to flower soon after germination. Flowering peaks by mid-summer and seeds drop before the first frost. The plants will begin to flower without being regulated by the light cycle. This characteristic seems to be dominant and is easily transferred to hybrids. Very often hybrids will have a small percentage of plants that are not autoflowering. Although flowering is not initiated by shorter days, flower growth is stimulated if there is some light deprivation, as few as 8 or 10 hours a day of uninterrupted darkness can increase flower growth considerably. Usually these plants go from germination to completion of flowering within 100–110 days.

With the many combinations and complex parentages of modern hybrids, it is impossible to generalize about the qualities of hybrids' smoke, highs, or other characteristics. So many plants have been crossed and their progeny used for breeding that it is truly a mixed-up world out there. The *Big Book of Buds* series answers your questions regarding characteristics of particular varieties.

The Buzz icon is the one that is most important to me. What is the high like? Describing a state of mind is not an easy task. Separating one's mental state from the state of mind created by the brain's interplay with cannabinoids is subtle. We have used many terms to describe this state:

active • alert • balanced • blissful • body relaxation • body stone • calm • cerebral • cheerful • clear (headed) • couchlock • creative • creeper • dreamy • energetic • euphoric • even head/body high • fast • functional • giggly • happy • hazy • heady • inspirational • intense • introspective • lively • lethargic • lucid • mellow • munchies • narcotic • pain relief • physically relaxing • playful • positive • psychedelic • sedative • sensual • sleepy • soaring • social • stoney • talkative • thoughtful • trippy • uplifting • visual • wandering mind

These descriptions attempt to capture the elusive qualities of the high and are based on a typical response; however, each person has a unique relationship with marijuana, which means his or her response to a strain may range outside of the typical. The text contains more complete descriptions.

The Taste/Smell icon is a short one to three word description of the smell and taste. Some of the odors included are:

acrid • berry • bubblegum • candy • chocolate • citrus • coffee • creamy • earthy • floral • fruit • hashy • herbal • honey • incense • mango • melon • musky • nutty • peppery • pine • pineapple • piney • pungent • sandalwood • skunk • smooth • spicy • sweet • tobacco • tropical sweet • vanilla • woodsy

The Flowering Time icon details the number of days it takes the plant to ripen after forcing flowering. Some outdoor strains also offer the approximate time of harvest. Both environmental conditions and subjective factors affect maturation.

Take, for instance, one experiment in which identical plants grown indoors in a lab were fed different water-soluble commercial fertilizers. These identical plants grown under identical conditions except the fertilizers ripened up to 10 days apart. The fertilizers also affected the taste and quality of the buds.

Plant growth and maturation is also affected by temperature. Both cold and hot conditions interfere with ripening. Temperate conditions encourage fast growth and prompt ripening. The planting method is another factor that affects ripening time. Hydroponic plants mature earlier than their sisters in planting medium.

I would call a plant ripe when the "resin" in the glands starts to turn milky or amber. This is about a week later than some people prefer. The taste differs and the cannabinoids may change a bit, resulting in different highs. Dutch coffee shops often sell bud that is immature. The glands are there, but have not filled completely with THC. The high is racing and buzzy. I don't find it that satisfying. Obviously, ripening time is affected by your idea of ripeness.

It is easy to see that the numbers mentioned are intended to give the reader an approximation rather than hard figures. While they offer an indication of what you should expect, they shouldn't be used to figure your timetable.

The Yield icon is a report of expected yield. These figures are somewhat ambiguous since the results are not reported consistently. Cannabis, like all green plants, uses light to fuel photosynthesis. The sugars produced become tissue. As a shortcut, you could say Light = Growth. Yields vary first and foremost due to light conditions, so space or plant definitions are incomplete by themselves. The yields that appear here assume that indoor gardens are receiving at least 600 watts per meter (wpm) where no light wattage is indicated.

The Parents icon is the parentage of the variety. While this can get quite complex, you get an idea of what the possibilities are for any variety by knowing its parents.

Some of the hybrids in the book are F2 unstabilized. When pure strains (let's call them strains A & B) are crossed and a hybrid is produced, the first generation, the F1 hybrid plants, are all uniform because they all contain the same genes. One set from the female and one set from the male. When two F1's are crossed, the seeds receive a random assortment of genes. For each of the more than 100,000 sets of genes, a plant may get two genes from A, one each from A and B, or two from B. No two plants are alike.

To stabilize them so that they have similar characteristics, the plants are inbred for five or six generations creating an F6, using careful selections. However breeders often work with unstabilized hybrids, which has an advantage when breeding for cloning.

Stability can be judged in part by the number of parents a variety has. Pure strains are the most uniform, since they are not recombining different genetic dispositions. Hybrids have the advantage of gaining vigor from the fresh combination. They also vary more. Strains with three or four parents are likely to exhibit more than one phenotype when grown out. When the three parents are hybrids themselves, the combination can result in quite a bit of diversity.

Diversity is not bad. Consider a gardener starting out. Clones are taken once the plants grow some side stems. When the plants have been harvested and tasted the gardener decides to select two plants for the next garden. Clones of those plants are grown vegetatively and used for mothers. If the seed line were uniform as it is with pure strains or stabilized varieties, there would not be much difference between the plants. Seeds from an unstabilized variety give the gardener more choices.

The following icons indicate recommendations for planting. The choices are:

 indoor

 outdoor

 indoor/outdoor

Outdoor strains may do well in a greenhouse setup, but will be difficult to grow indoors. They may require too much light for inside growing, and usually have their own ideas about growth and height, making them hard to tame. The problem with most plants not recommended for outdoors in temperate climates is the plants don't ripen by the end of the season. Some plants rated as indoor plants can be grown outdoors if they are forced to flower early using shade cloth. As an example, a plant which ripens in mid-November, 45 days after a gardener's September 30th harvest schedule, could be coaxed to flower early by covering it with opaque plastic each evening after sunset. Remove the cover 12 hours after sunset,

beginning in late spring or early summer. Most varieties will ripen within 60–70 days.

Plants that are recommended for growing outdoors indicate the maturity date under natural light. When no latitude is mentioned, figure the month indicated is at the same latitude as the country of origin. For Holland, the latitude is 52° N. Canadian seeds are produced at the 50° N latitude, U.S. seeds at the 38° N latitude, and Spanish seeds are produced at the 40–41° N latitude. More can be learned about outdoor harvest times and latitude in the appendixes. Also read Franco's article on drying and curing (page 108) to discover how these processes influence the flavor and the high.

This icon only appears on varieties that have been feminized. Feminized seeds are the result of a cross between a regular female and male induced pollen on a second female, resulting in 100% female seeds. Feminized seeds are great for the gardener that does not want to sex plants. Breeders may want a mix of male and female seeds for their purposes. Some varieties are only available in a feminized form, while other breeders offer both regular and feminized versions of the same strains to suit the needs of different gardening projects.

This icon only appears on varieties that are autoflowering. While most varieties of domesticated marijuana fall into the major categories of indica or sativa, the autoflowering ruderalis subspecies has become more common.

As any cannabis gardener knows, a main aspect of cannabis cultivation with sativa and indica strains is flower forcing. Normally plants must be forced to enter flowering, which means to begin forming buds. This is accomplished by changing the light cycle so that plants get 10–12 hours of uninterrupted darkness. This light cycle mimics outdoor conditions, since days get longer (and the night darkness shorter) until the summer solstice on June 22, after which the days shorten through the remainder of the summer and fall. The difference in light-hours from summer to winter depends in part on latitude. Close to the equator, both weather and light-hours vary less from summer to winter. The differences in both light hours and seasonal weather are more dramatic as one moves north or south in latitude.

Until recently, gardeners had to plan for the dark period carefully. For outdoor growers, this meant selecting varieties that would be forced to flower early enough to finish in their location, or to plan to block light to outdoor plants using covering. Indoor gardeners needed to ensure the room had no light leaks and plan garden tending around the light cycle. While these are still good measures to take, autoflowering varieties reduce the requirements to strictly control the light and dark cycles.

Autoflowering strains instead take their cue to flower based on how long they have been growing rather than how much uninterrupted darkness they receive. Autoflowering varieties bring a new versatility to growing, allowing plants to flourish in environments where light pollution would have created difficulties. They also make plants a little easier for new growers who do not have to master the light regimen or monitor it strictly in order to grow a successful crop.

SOG This icon is listed only on plants suitable for sea of green gardens. Plants in these gardens are spaced together very closely so that each plant needs to grow little if any to fill the canopy. Plants are forced to flower soon after they are placed in the flowering space. Eliminating the vegetative growth stage decreases turnaround. SOG gardens hold 3 to 6 plants per square foot.

This icon is listed only on plants suitable for screen of green gardens. There are many different versions of screen of green, or SCROG. The one thing these methods have in common is that they use a screen to support buds, allowing for denser bud growth. This can be done both horizontally and vertically. This situation often happens when plants of different varieties are being cultivated. The problem with this technique is that while the topside of the buds receives plenty of light, the undersides do not. See the screen of green by Franco on page 166 for more information.

Once again, fuller descriptions are found within the descriptive text for each variety. The icons are fast reference points. They give you an idea of where the story is going. The accompanying variety description provides more nuanced details and tips about the plant's preferences. Still, we have to admit that we love the photos the most. They show what words can only attempt to express. I'm sure they will provide you with hours of sightseeing pleasure.

Photo: Justin McIvor

A-Train • Afghanica • AK 47 • American Dream Lights • Aurora B. • Barney's Farm Blue Cheese God Bud • BC Sweet Tooth • Big Bang • Big B Cheese • Blueberry • Bubble Cheese • Buddh Chronic • Double Dutch • Dr. Grinspoon • Dutc Super Bud • First Lady • Flo • Fruit of the Gods • Hashberry • Hawaiian Snow • Headband • I Jack the Ripper • Jacky White • Jilly Bean • K • Léda Uno • Lemon Skunk • Lowryder #2 • L • Mazar • Medicine Man • Morning Glory • Mo Diesel • Northern Lights • Northern Lights-H Power Plant • Querkle • Sage • Skunk Haze • Super Lemon Haze • Super Silver Haze • Ta The Pure Skunk #1 • The Purps • The Ultima • White Rhino • White Russian • Wh

Amnesia Haze • Arctic Sun •Atomic Northern
• Barney's Farm GI3 Haze • BC Blueberry • BC
d • Big Buddha Cheese • Black Domina • Blue
Haze • California Indica • Cheesus • Chiesel •
en's Royal Orange • Easy Rider • Ed Rosenthal
ruity Thai • G Bomb • Grape Kush • Hash Plant
• Iranian Autoflower • Jack F6 • Jack Herer •
Mist • Kalichakra • Kushage •LA Confidential

Varieties

• Mango • Master K
ation • Nebula • Nevil's Haze • New York City
e • NYPD • Orange Bud • Pineapple Punch •
rawberry Cough • Strawberry Haze (Arjan's)
e Gold • The Church • The Doctor • The Kali •
Vanilla Kush • Vortex • Wappa • White Berry
Satin • White Smurf • White Widow

A-Train

TH Seeds

 50/50

 euphoric, clear-headed

 menthol, lemon, hashy

 53-60 days

 Arcata Trainwreck ♀ x Mazar-i-Sharif Afghan ♂

 25-35 g/plant SOG, 50-90 g/plant in 5-gal. pots

All aboard! The A-Train is about to take you on a journey from the rolling hills of northern California through the Mazar-i-Sharif mountains of Afghanistan, finally arriving in the Low Countries of Europe. This California-Afghani F1 hybrid was bred in Holland for indoor grows. A-Train's father comes from Afghanistan's hash heartland, while her California mom is Trainwreck, a clone-only variety from the West Coast medical marijuana community renowned for an excellent high and refreshing flavor.

A-Train performs best as a multi-branch plant. She is a space hog, with extensive lower branching and a tendency to sprawl and lean. Supports or netting are recommended for those who want their girls to be orderly. If allowed to grow without control, her branches will probably still need rearranging in order to maximize light for the buds. No matter how she is trained, it is advisable to trim off the lower branches, reserving energy for bud formations on her upper levels.

Gardeners who prioritize yield should consider hydroponics for this strain, while those in search of primo flavors do better with soil. Either way, A-Train loves organic foods. When growing hydroponically, TH Seeds prefers Botanicare Pure Blend Pro and Liquid Karma to pump up the enzymes. During peak flowering times, they use Bud Swell. A-Train will become finicky and troublesome if exposed to too much humidity. Otherwise, she is a clean, dry, and relatively non-smelly plant.

This strain finishes in 7½ to 8½ weeks. She more than quadruples in height during that time, starting when she is forced – beginning the flowering cycle at one foot (30 cm) will result in plants that are 4½ to 5 feet (1.3 to 1.5m) at finish. As she grows, this lanky brancher takes on a gauzy green coloration, and tends to form many plantlet buds. If she is pruned to a single-cola plant, A-Train will produce 25-35 grams (approx. 1 oz.) per plant. When grown in 1-gallon containers in soil, she yields 35-55 grams per plant, and 5-gallon potted plants can deliver between 50 and 90 grams (2-3 oz.) apiece.

The harvested buds are round and compact, resembling clusters of green walnuts coated with a silver shellac of resin. On the menthol-lemon inhale, A-Train brings you a satisfying, well balanced mind and body lift, a clear and and productive high. On the exhale of lip-numbing sweetness with bits of Afghan hashiness, A-Train brings you home; you can drop your baggage from the day. This strain's creeper high will gradually slow you down a notch or two, but it won't stun you into a stupor. It's a combination of two strains used widely by the medical pot community for alleviating mind and body discomfort.

Afghanica
Flying Dutchmen

Photo: Cannabis College

Afghanica is an F1 hybrid that is true to its roots. This predominantly indica plant grows short and stocky, with broad leaves and a thick canopy. Afghanica produces well when gardened inside or outdoors in most temperate regions, but yields are heaviest when it is grown in a sea of green (12-16 plants psm or 3-4 plants psf). Trim away lower branches before the onset of flowering; this allows the plant to devote all available energy to the light-immersed tops. Removing lower branches outdoors late in the season also increases airflow, limiting potential mold or pest problems.

In a normal season, Afghanica matures into a 6-foot (2-meter) tall Christmas tree, and may exhibit red or purple coloration in colder climates. No matter where she is grown, organic soil will foster a sweeter, more refined end product. Afghanica has low-to-medium nutrient requirements. Too many nutrients in the latter stages of maturation impair the taste. No nutrients should be given for the last 10 days before harvest. Although this strain often looks ready well before its 8-9 weeks of flowering are finished, the yield and potency increase tremendously in the last week. It is worth the wait.

When nearing harvest, Afghanica plants emit a petrol-type aroma at the slightest disturbance. The buds are fairly dense and very oily throughout. The coated smaller leaves are worth collecting, as they produce an abundance of heavy, oily resin when put through a screen. Smell and taste are typical Afghani—acrid, pungent and volatile, although the Skunk father lends a little sweetness. The high is potent, lethargic and physical in nature. It comes on slowly and has a longlasting depth and density. If smoked late at night the effects can often still be felt in the morning. Medicinally, Afghanica is effective relief for insomnia and chronic pain.

 62.5/37.5

 physical, lethargic

 acrid, pungent

 56-63 days indoors
mid-Oct. outdoors

 ♀ Afghani #1 (P1) x
♂ Original Skunk #1 (P1)

 1 g per watt of light indoors

 SOG

AK-47

Serious Seeds

Photo: A. Grossmann

Despite its aggressive name, AK-47 has many peaceful tendencies. First bred in 1992, the name suggests the power packed in its dark, resinous, compact buds that bristle with red hairs and glistening trichomes. AK-47 has a spiced aroma bordering on skunk, with a hint of sandalwood, but tastes sweeter and more floral than the smell would lead one to expect.

AK has mostly sativa characteristics with one exception: a quick finishing time. This variety was reworked in 1999 to increase stability, so results from seeds are uniform. A tall plant with substantial girth and big fat calyxes, she performs excellently in indoor environments, both soil and hydro, and has been grown outdoors with good results in Spain. In low to medium temperatures this variety produces a denser bud; in high temperatures buds are fluffier and more open, but total yields are roughly equivalent.

The AK-47 buzz is immediate and long lasting with an alert but mellow cerebral effect. Lab tests have rated the THC content at over 20 percent, making it a "one hit wonder" for many smokers. This variety can be a little spacey, but is great for playing and listening to music, or other social activities with friends. AK-47 helped put Serious Seeds on the map with a 2nd place finish in the hydroponics competition and a 3rd place in the overall category at the 1995 Cannabis Cup in the Netherlands. Overall, AK-47 has won 7 awards.

 65/35

 cerebral, alert, munchies

 woodsy smell/ sweet taste

 63-70 days indoors

 Colombian, Mexican, Thai & Afghani

 500 g per m2

31

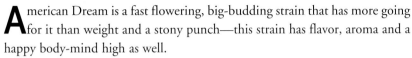

American Dream
Sensi Seed Bank

American Dream is a fast flowering, big-budding strain that has more going for it than weight and a stony punch—this strain has flavor, aroma and a happy body-mind high as well.

American Dream performs reliably for first-time growers in a range of conditions, overcoming any number of small imperfections and still producing a harvest of potent, fragrant flowers. In the hands of a more experienced grower, American Dream can really shine, and should be a breath of fresh air to anyone who thinks that all new hybrids are the same. An ideal plant for indoors, American Dream is very responsive to training and an excellent choice for the sea of green (SOG) method because she gains more height than a pure indica, but will not grow out of control when flowered at normal SOG sizes. She can be trained to stay small or allowed to grow into a large plant with multiple stems. In warm climates or greenhouses, this plant flourishes, with mature outdoor heights reaching 4 to 8 feet (125-250 cm).

The skunk heritage is evident in this plant's structure and growth patterns. American Dream has strong stems, short internode gaps and a fast, powerful indica-type growth at all stages. Mid-stem branches can grow nearly as tall as her central cola and may need support in late flowering as the buds start to gain bulk. Sativa influences can be seen in the calyx/bud formation and are present in the THC content. Individual tops are dense and fat, creating an interesting pyramid shape as they form—their round, oversized calyxes bubble up to a blunt peak, and the way they stack atop each other gives the appearance of three or four triangular, almost-flat surfaces leading to the apex. When these polygonal chunks grow, they coalesce into long, thick cylinders of dewy bud. Small growths pop out from the main cola at every angle like kernels of corn popping on the cob. The medium green of these buds is glazed with a thick, quicksilver sheen of resin, making them terrific for hash hopefuls or cannabis cooks. Processing buds and small leaves will yield a significant amount of superb hashish, but even growers who don't take this step can salvage plenty of finger hash during the manicure.

American Dream's citrusy high comes on like the proverbial ton of bricks. Normal consumption should not be incapacitating for the average smoker, but it might be a better strain in familiar and stress-free surroundings. The effect is less up or down, than sideways. Neither hyper nor sleepy, American Dream tends to simply shift things into a new perspective that increases a feeling of being "in the moment," making it an enhancement for getting caught up in a film, book, music or video game.

 70/30

 talkative, happy

 citrus skunk

 45-50 days/mid-Oct.

♀Afghani Skunk x ♂ SP intermed/ NL#5 line

100g/indoor plant grown to 100-125cm

 greenhouse outdoor below 45°N latitude

American Dream

We named this variety "American Dream" because a room or garden full of these ladies is a beautiful expression of life, liberty and the pursuit of happiness, even if the plants themselves are forbidden under the current interpretation of that creed.

The American Dream is built on beliefs like self-improvement and self-reliance; a person's inherent right to do what they wish, provided it harms no one else; the idea that the most modest beginnings can blossom into bountiful rewards through the application of honest work.

The American Dream seed strain is named because it, along with all lovingly-grown cannabis around the world, represents and embodies those values so well.

Amnesia Haze
Soma's Sacred Seeds

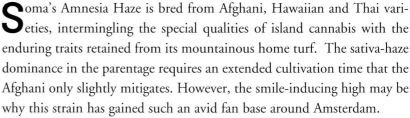

Soma's Amnesia Haze is bred from Afghani, Hawaiian and Thai varieties, intermingling the special qualities of island cannabis with the enduring traits retained from its mountainous home turf. The sativa-haze dominance in the parentage requires an extended cultivation time that the Afghani only slightly mitigates. However, the smile-inducing high may be why this strain has gained such an avid fan base around Amsterdam.

Outdoors, Amnesia Haze likes the tropics; indoors, she needs an experienced hand, and prefers a roomy space, or better yet, a greenhouse. She does equally well in soil and hydro, although Soma prefers soil fertilized with guano and other organic products.

Haze is tall, expansive, and likes to branch out, forming more calyx than leaf. Her few leaves start off thick and green but look like purple crinkled paper by harvest. The blooms start small and slowly accumulate many promising white hairs during her 13-week indoor flowering cycle. By the finish, this strain's trichome hairs are unusually lengthy. Each plant rewards the diligent gardener with yields of up to 50 grams (1¾ ounces) of high end bud.

The Thai/Haze heritage lends a clean, slightly orange taste and a high that reminds users of the first time they got ripped smoking Thai stick. The texture of this experience builds slowly to a euphoric forgetfulness suitable for partying. The name of this variety comes from its ability to induce an intense buzz that often fragments short-term memory momentarily, and users should bear this in mind before undertaking any tasks that rely on a fluid connectedness of one's thoughts. Amnesia Haze may relieve chronic pain and inflammatory conditions like multiple sclerosis. In 2004, she won 1st place in the First Annual International Cannagraphic Growers' Cup in Amsterdam.

 70/30

 creeper, euphoric

 Thai stick

 90-95 days indoors
end Nov. outdoors

 ♀ Afghani-Hawaiian
x ♂ Southeast Asian

 40-50 g (11/2-2 oz.)
per plant indoors

Arctic Sun
Flying Dutchmen

Arctic Sun is a combination of two powerhouses of the Dutch seed-breeding establishment—Skunk #1 and White Widow—which have been used extensively in Holland to create high yielding, potent strains. The White Widow mother has been in Flying Dutchmen's library for over a decade. Originally a South Indian/Brazilian hybrid, the mother plant boasts a 12-week maturation time, extreme potency and a high yield. Crossing this strain with a strong skunk father produces a 60/40 sativa/indica plant that can be grown indoors in a greenhouse or outdoors at a latitude below 40 degrees North.

Indoors this plant gives the best results when grown without pruning at a density of 12-16 plants per square meter. Trimming off all the lower shoots at the base of the plants allows for more airflow and focuses the growth at the top. Arctic Sun usually finishes with a central calyx and 6-8 side branches, at a height of around 2-2¾ feet (60-80 cm) with the lowest 1 foot (30 cm) bare. The usual yields are 1½ -1¾ ounces (40-50 g) per plant at 600 watts of light per square meter.

After testing Arctic Sun in most mediums, Flying Dutchmen recommends growing in pre-dressed soil high in organic matter, although high quality yields are also common in coco fiber and rockwool. Arctic Sun has a fairly dense growth pattern during vegetative growth, with short internode spaces and medium-dark green, mid-sized leaflets and longish petioles, maturing into short to medium height plants with compact buds that have large bracts and few pistils.

Outdoors the unpruned Arctic Sun matures into a stocky 6-foot (2.5 m) Christmas tree with occasional purple coloration. Yields outdoors can be spectacular during a good season; greenhouse plants have weighed in at 22-24 ounces (650-700 g) per plant in Holland. Artic Sun thrives on fairly high nutrient levels. Special care should be taken to flush plants in the last 10-14 days for optimum taste. Although some plants in the population finish at 8 weeks, the nicest plants for selection tend to be fully mature at 9 weeks. In Holland, Arctic Sun matures at the end of October.

At harvest, Arctic Sun has an aroma that is balanced between her parents: a pungent fuel-like tang with surprising floral undertones. The buds are dense, greasy and very heavy. When cured, the buds mellow a little, leaving a perfect balance of potency and everyday enjoyability. Tastewise, the curry house pungency is tempered by the sweetness of the Skunk #1. The Artic Sun is loved by smokers with high tolerance levels. The high is both cerebral and physical and can be enjoyed over time without developing a threshold. The cannabinoid profile of the Artic Sun lends itself well to medical applications for chronic pain, spasms associated with MS and sleeplessness.

 60/40

 even head/body high

 fuel, floral

 56-70 days/end Oct.

 ♀ White Widow (P1) x ♂ Skunk #1 (P1)

 1 g/watt of light used

 below 40°N latitude greenhouse

Atomic Northern Lights
Dr. Atomic

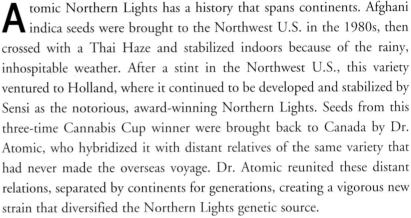

Atomic Northern Lights has a history that spans continents. Afghani indica seeds were brought to the Northwest U.S. in the 1980s, then crossed with a Thai Haze and stabilized indoors because of the rainy, inhospitable weather. After a stint in the Northwest U.S., this variety ventured to Holland, where it continued to be developed and stabilized by Sensi as the notorious, award-winning Northern Lights. Seeds from this three-time Cannabis Cup winner were brought back to Canada by Dr. Atomic, who hybridized it with distant relatives of the same variety that had never made the overseas voyage. Dr. Atomic reunited these distant relations, separated by continents for generations, creating a vigorous new strain that diversified the Northern Lights genetic source.

Atomic Northern Lights shows its indica heritage in its growth characteristics, producing a short stocky plant that has a relatively quick flowering time. The buzz has a wider bandwidth than the typical indica-dominant variety, providing a balanced mind and body high that has an overall uplifting effect. Atomic Northern Lights is a smooth smoke with a sweet pungent flavor.

This classic, evergreen-tree-shaped plant is not too branchy and works well as "pole pot," staked with one center cola and up to four side colas that are smaller. If trimmed properly, Atomic Northern Lights works well in a sea of green. Dr. Atomic prefers soil growing methods, but this hardy plant will give satisfying results in most gardening set-ups.

 65/35

 even head-body

 sweet and pungent

 50-65 days in mid-Oct out

 stable hybrids from Holland & Northwest U.S.

 100 g per plant in 400 g per plant out

 SOG

Aurora B.
Flying Dutchmen

Aurora Borealis is the Latin name for the natural phenomena at the North Pole otherwise known as "Northern Lights," which in turn is the name of one of this plant's celebrity parents. Northern Lights is an indica strain that, during the 1980s, made its way from the Pacific Northwest to the Netherlands, where it has become a building block for many strains around the world. The Northern Lights #10 mother was selected for commercial production back in 1997. While Northern Lights was specifically bred for the then-fledgling indoor grow scene, the other parent in this famous pair, Skunk #1, was initially bred for outdoors and greenhouse cultivation. The resulting plants are of a medium height, with dark green foliage and short internodes and a 50/50 sativa/indica phenotype expression. Aurora Borealis may have a less recognizable name than her parents, but her genetics shine through to reveal her family ties.

This strain can be grown in all suitable mediums and will thrive in most temperate regions. Outdoors, in Holland, the Aurora B. matures in mid-October. She comes up stocky with dark green foliage. Plants started in May in Holland, and left unpruned, usually finish at a height of around 5-6 feet (1.5-2 m). They yield around 300 grams per plant, weather permitting. Greenhouse yields are higher, surpassing 500 grams per plant.

Indoors, the Aurora B. performs best under a sea of green regime at a density of 16-25 plants per square meter. She thrives on generous nutrient levels and performs best in a good, rich, well aerated soil high in organic matter. Allow for a vegetative time of around 10 days or until the canopy cover is about 70% when viewed from above. Do not prune that canopy unless a longer vegetation time is required. All feeding should cease during the last 10 days of flowering so as not to impair the taste of the final product. The height of Aurora Borealis under this regime is usually around 1-2 feet (40-60 cms) and its yield ranges from 25 to 40 grams per plant, at 600 watts of light per square meter.

Once the plants mature they exhibit fairly long, broad colas with a medium density and very high resin content. The smell and taste is satisfyingly sweet, with a warm skunky undertone. The plants' odor is very pungent until fully dried and cured. Aurora B.'s high leans toward the physical, starting strong, with a long lasting and well balanced plateau and a gentle finish. Medicinally, this strain works well to alleviate symptoms for which indicas are generally prescribed, such as chronic pain, spasms, sleeplessness and nausea.

 50/50

 gentle body high

 sweet, skunky

 56-63 days/ mid-Oct.

 ♀ Northern Lights 10 (P1) x ♂ Skunk #1 (P1)

 1 gram/watt of light used

 greenhouse

 SOG

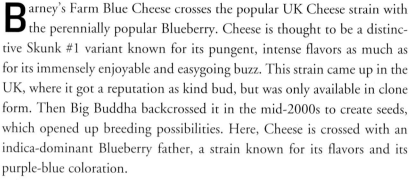

Barney's Farm Blue Cheese
Barney's Farm

Barney's Farm Blue Cheese crosses the popular UK Cheese strain with the perennially popular Blueberry. Cheese is thought to be a distinctive Skunk #1 variant known for its pungent, intense flavors as much as for its immensely enjoyable and easygoing buzz. This strain came up in the UK, where it got a reputation as kind bud, but was only available in clone form. Then Big Buddha backcrossed it in the mid-2000s to create seeds, which opened up breeding possibilities. Here, Cheese is crossed with an indica-dominant Blueberry father, a strain known for its flavors and its purple-blue coloration.

When selectively crossed, these two distinct tasting and widely recognized varieties have resulted in an incredibly fragrant and easy to grow strain. Barney's Farm Blue Cheese likes to shoot up long and straight, forming a thick main stem. The side branching is significant and forms a strong tree-like frame that can be easily trained to a screen of green. This plant stays short and stocky, finishing in 9–10 weeks with highly productive yields of tight, sticky spear-shaped colas. Buds are light green and springy to the touch, with pale orange hairs jutting out of elongated calyxes. Average yields are 1.5–2 ounces (45–60g) per plant.

Barney's Farm Blue Cheese is a variety with a one-of-a-kind taste—it is rich, round, and smooth, with a connoisseur's spectrum from the sweet and floral to the deep, earthen chocolate baseline. The intense and pungent earthy musk aromas of the Cheese are retained, but are now tempered with sweet incense-like Blueberry notes. The Barney's Farm Blue Cheese high is very heady. It creeps up then comes on strong and indica, with a full body stone. Many people will enjoy the trajectory of this mentally peaceful and physically relieving buzz. It has a pleasant entry and exit, although as it winds down, some people might find it a bit of a knockout, requiring a short nap to reset before moving on to any other activity.

I

calm, relaxing

berries and cream

60–70 days

♀ Skunk #1 Cheese variant x ♂ Blueberry

45-60g per plant in

in preferred

Barney's Farm GI3-Haze

Barney's Farm

Barney's Farm G-13 Haze is an award-winning variety that crosses the legendary G-13 with Barney's Farm's favorite Hawaiian sativa. G-13 is a strain of mythic proportions because of its alleged origins in the experimental U.S. medical marijuana compassionate access program. This federal program provided medical cannabis to a small select group of patients. It started in the late 1970s, but when activists organized a flood of applications for HIV/AIDS patients to enter the program in the early 1990s, the government panicked and closed the program to new entrants.

Some have said that any government-grown weed could only be low-grade, but others insist that the government program's scientific approach resulted in the creation of a superstrain: G-13. Rumors circulated in the 1990s claiming that a G-13 clone had been smuggled from the grow facility. Shortly thereafter breeders had backcrossed the G-13 into seed form and the name began to crop up all over the map. In the Barney's Farm cross, G-13 has been combined with a great tasting island sativa that has strong haze influences in composition. Straight out of the gate, Barney's Farm G-13 Haze has a very nice smell of ripe fruit and haze-sandalwood spiciness.

This variety is best compared with other sativa-dominant and haze plants. In general, haze hybrids require the vegetative time to be kept short. Flower forcing for this variety is recommended as soon as the clones have had a chance to establish themselves, which is helpful given that flowering times are fairly long, taking 10–12 weeks to ripen.

When vegged as directed, Barney's Farm G-13 Haze maintains a medium-tall stature with sturdy branches. This plant grows vigorously, and the flower structure has better density than many hazes, resulting in an above-average yield. The size and sturdiness of the plants also make it easier to grow in restricted indoor spaces than the typical haze. The buds have a bit of sativa sponginess to them, but this plant likes to form one large main cola on the central branch. This tendency makes it ideal for a SOG garden, although SCROG is another good choice. Not only does G-13 Haze offer healthy yields with good THC levels, it also possesses intense aromas and flavors and a powerful cerebral smoke worth savoring. This variety encapsulates the winning qualities of flavor and high that many sativa lovers seek out, but maintains a bass note of indica that anchors the effects nicely. Barney's Farm G-13 Haze has had multiple wins at the High Times Cannabis Cup, taking 2nd place in 2006, and 1st place in 2007.

 soaring, cerebral

 fruity haze

 70–80 days

 G-13 x Hawaiian sativa

 500g per m2

 in preferred

 SOG

BC Blueberry
BC Bud Depot

Photos: JamJakin & BC Bud Depot

This strain was created by BC Bud Depot to make a renowned British Columbia clone—the only blueberry plant available in seed form. They crossed the clone plant with an unknown blueberry seed father, resulting in a mostly indica plant that is deliciously fruity sweet with just a hint of fuel.

The BC Blueberry is a moderate brancher, forming the typical triangular shape. She can also be pruned at the transition to flowering, making a nice sea of green plant. She is particular about her conditions, which makes her more appropriate for gardeners with a little experience or a good intuitive sense for adjusting conditions. With the right care, this variety performs admirably in either indoor or outdoor gardens, with an 8-9 week flowering time. Outdoors, BC Blueberry can be grown in temperate regions as long as weather does not turn before the harvesting date, around the middle of September. While this plant can be grown in any medium, soil will bring out her luscious flavors. Yields average 1.5 to 2.5 ounces (40-70g) per plant when grown indoors, or between 4 and 16 ounces (115-450g) in outdoor gardens, depending on growing conditions and vegetative times.

While three-quarters of these plants will be green, one-quarter are a phenotype that features blue tones and pink hairs. Both phenotypes have medium-thick leaves. BC Blueberry is nutrient sensitive and is a dainty eater, so growers should take care to not overfeed these plants. She can also be sensitive to overly wet conditions. At finish plants grow to 3 or 4 feet (1-1.3m), making them good for rooms with space limitations. Outdoors, they will average nearly double their indoor heights.

With some TLC, BC Blueberry rewards the hobby grower with compact sweet smelling blueberry buds that are coated with creamy resinous glands. When cured, the buds will turn blue. The effect of BC Blueberry is blissful. The high creeps into a pleasant and awake state that is very functional. Compared to many varieties, BC Blueberry's high is relatively short, but comforting and tasty.

 80/20

 calm, dreamy, munchies

 fruit and fuel

 55-63 days

 longtime BC Blueberry clone ♀ x unknown ♂

 100 g/plant in; 1000 g/plant out

BC God Bud
BC Bud Depot

Photo: Isabella

The memorably-named God Bud rose from underground fame in Canada's medical pot community to international acclaim when BC Bud Depot debuted her as a commercial strain in 2004. Her heavy yields and strong effect have made BC God Bud an indica worthy of praise.

BC God Bud is short, squat and dense, with plenty of silvery resin. While she does well outside in California, yielding up to 3 pounds (1.3 kg) per plant, she does not finish well as far north as British Columbia and is better for indoor cultivation in cool climates. Although BC God Bud can be hard on beginners, attentive growers will find this to be a hardy, pest resistant plant with leathery leaves and an appetite for nutrients. These plants require 8-10 weeks of flowering time to reach maturity. As the plants ripen, their dark greens turn to shades of purple, and a heady, almost high-inducing smell begins to fill the grow room, requiring some odor control precautions.

 75/25

 relaxing, dreamy, sedative

 lavender, tropical, pine

 55-70 days

 God Bud clone ♀ x Hawaiian Purple Indica ♂

 100-200g/plant

SOG

These plants stay at the shortest end of the growth spectrum, reaching only 2-3 feet (up to 1 m) in height at harvest, with a bud production that can maximize smaller spaces. While the BC God Bud is not a single-cola plant, her side branching is minimal enough to make it a good sea of green choice. Under these conditions, she can deliver a whopping 3-4 ounces (85-115 g) of compact, sparklingly resinous buds per plant.

On the toke, BC God Bud delivers a musky, tropical flavor with herbal edges and hints of lavender, berry, and pine. The high is well balanced, a slight creeper with longlasting effects, starting with a calm, pleasant feeling and increasing to a more surreal, nearly hallucinogenic buzz. She is good for general pain relief and makes a pleasant nighttime smoke. Her innerspace high flourishes in calm environments rather than loud nightclubs or high-stress social encounters. The peace of BC God Bud unfolds in the garden or at the drawing table, and in the quiet hours before bed.

1st Prize, Battle of the Bridges 2006 — A High Times Private Growers Competition, USA (NY) vs Canada (Ontario)
Named one of *High Times* Top 10 Strains of the Year, 2005
2nd prize International Cannagraphics 420 Cup, God Hash, 2005
1st Prize *High Times* Cannabis Cup – Best Indica, 2004

BC Sweet Tooth
BC Bud Depot

Photo: Isabella

This strain gets her name from her intense sugar on the palate, but just because she is sweet on the tongue does not mean she is dainty on the stone. The BC Sweet Tooth is a candy-coated bomb to the senses, not recommended for daytime functionality, but terrific for inducing sleep, soothing pain or indulging in languorous, mellow relaxation. The combination of medicinal-grade stone, big yields, and quick finishing time make this variety an excellent choice for impatient growers looking for a cavity-defying sweet indica.

BC Sweet Tooth finishes in 6-7 weeks, or by early to mid September in outdoor environments. This rapid schedule brings BC Sweet Tooth in before the frost in coastal British Columbia, or in locations south to the equator. Indoors, this variety can finish even faster, in as little as 40 days. BC Sweet Tooth branches moderately and can be easily manipulated to conform to either a multi-branch or sea of green gardening style.

A medium feeder that is good for beginners and connoisseurs alike, BC Sweet Tooth is a hardy plant that defends herself well against pests, but can show mold susceptibility if planted too late outdoors or raised in overly moist environments indoors. Her dense, nuggety buds look edible, and smell almost as sweet as they taste. BC Sweet Tooth's height at finish averages 3-4 feet (1 to 1.3 m) indoors or 6-8 feet (2-2.6 m) outdoors. Her average yields are 2.5-3.5 ounces (70-100 g) per plant in an indoor setup, or 4-16 ounces (115-450 g) outdoors, depending on the growing region and its conditions.

BC Sweet Tooth's syrupy buds are good medication for chronic pain, but less optimal for mixed crowds and socializing. This strain delivers a hammer to the head, and can be a day-wrecker if its effects are unanticipated. The high has a lasting effect, and can lead to couch-lock, but if a major body soothing sensation is desired, BC Sweet Tooth is a promising strain to seek out.

 90/10

 body ease, couchlock

 sweet, honey, citrus

 40-50 days

 BC Sweet Tooth #3 ♀ x Sweet Tooth #3 and BC Sweet Tooth IBL ♂

 100 g/plant in SOG; 1500 g/plant out

 SOG

Marijuana: The Amazing Plant

This illustration by K. Abellán deconstructs the mysterious botany of the cannabis plant from seed to maturity. The lingo for marijuana's botanical components are sometimes familiar and sometimes strangely scientific. A truly amazing plant, cannabis is the only known dioecious (gendered) annual in the plant kingdom.

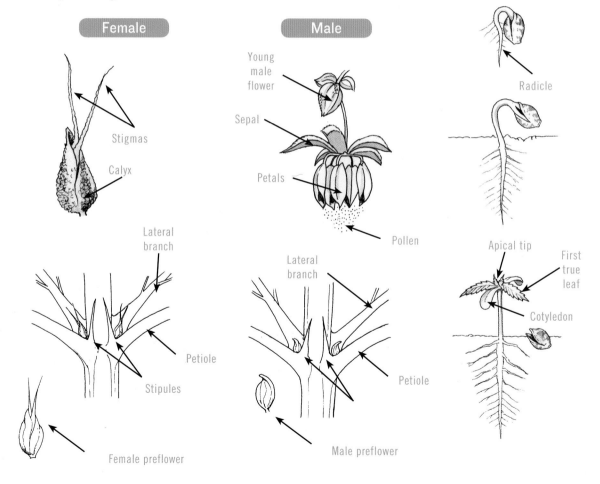

Female

Male

Stigmas

Calyx

Young male flower

Sepal

Petals

Pollen

Radicle

Lateral branch

Lateral branch

Petiole

Apical tip

First true leaf

Cotyledon

Stipules

Petiole

Female preflower

Male preflower

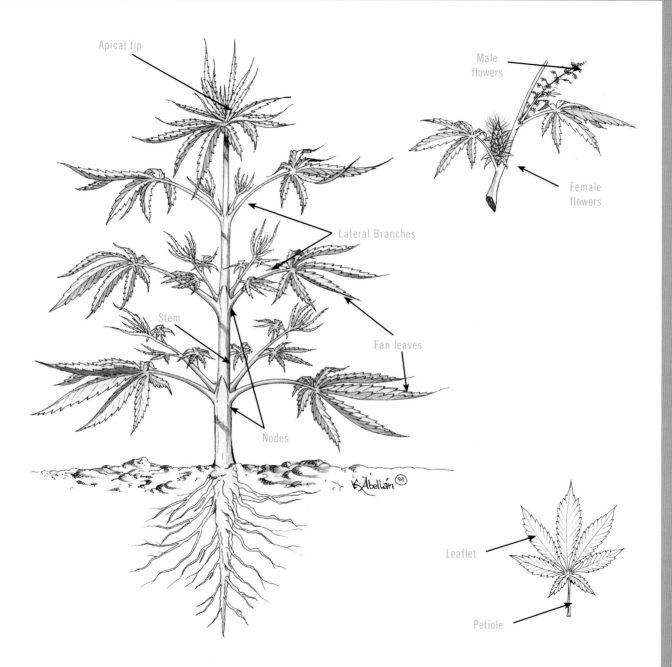

Apical tip

Lateral Branches

Stem

Fan leaves

Nodes

Male flowers

Female flowers

Leaflet

Petiole

K. Abellán '98

Big Bang

Green House Seed Company

The Big Bang is a strong, explosive indica, ideal in 5-gallon (20 L) containers, as well as for SOG or SCROG systems. This fast, compact plant forms a plump firework of a bush. Big Bang can take a lot of feeding, and will pop out some very smelly buds that can give your air filters a run for their money.

Best results are obtained in a hydroponics system, although Big Bang will also do well in soil. If this plant is allowed to grow large, its strong branching and short internode lengths will require some pruning to allow more light and air to reach the inner and lower branches. Growers should start this variety with a medium-low pH (5.6 hydro / 5.8 soil) and slowly increase to reach 6.5 at the end of flowering. EC levels depend on the system. The maximum EC should be 2.0 in hydro and 1.8 in soil. Adequate flushing should be provided. Plants in 5 gallon containers will reach 4-5 feet at harvest if grown for at least 2 weeks. Plants in smaller containers reach 2-3 feet. With no limit to root development, and ideal conditions, Big Bang can skyrocket to over 7 feet in height.

Big Bang forms small round buds with overlapping clusters of calyxes, and thick short hairs. Although her leaves are bright green, her resin dulls the color with its grayish shade. Her medium-sized leaflets tend to overlap.

Aside from describing her bursting growth, the name Big Bang also describes this strain's stone, which comes on strong and very smooth, with a semi-narcotic medicinal effect. Like a healing nova within the body, the high expands throughout the system to release tension and pain and create a soothing state. The effect is steady and longlasting. Big Bang's flavor is very intense and sweet, reminiscent of apple, rose and violet candies. Known for her medicinal properties, Big Bang is chosen by thousands of medicinal users in Holland, where it is known as "Simm-18." This strain is good as a muscle relaxer for multiple sclerosis and helps alleviate chronic pain. Big Bang will also be enjoyed recreationally by those seeking a physically relaxing effect. Big Bang won 3rd Prize in the *High Times* Cannabis Cup, 2000.

 80/20

 physical, muscle relaxation

 sweet, rose, violet, apple

 63 days/early Oct.

 ♀ Skunk/Northern Lights x ♂ El Nino

 up to 700 g/m2 in; up to 1000 g/plant out

 SOG

Big Bud
Sensi Seed Bank

Photo: Jan Otsen

Big Bud is a classic favorite, and with good reason. This plant has traits that so many marijuana growers and enthusiasts are after: prodigious growth and a desirable high. Already a part of the Seed Bank breeding program in the 1980s, Big Bud was first sold as a hybrid with Skunk #1 from the Sacred Seed Company. This is the version that claimed the 1989 win in the mostly indica category at the Cannabis Cup. In the 1990s, Sensi Seeds and the Seed Bank merged and new attention was given to this hybrid. Another sweet, high-yielding, heavily indica line was crossed into the original hybrid, making this plant-type sweeter and more delicious to connoisseurs. With the new burst of flavor, the strain became interesting for more than just its heavy yields, which resulted in a fully unexpected prize for Big Bud in the 1996 Cannabis Cup.

As the name suggests, this variety is a producer: it is a good idea to tie up bottom branches because they may break due to the weight. A large internode ratio means that this variety requires minimal pruning to get maximum light to the flowers and makes an easy job of manicuring at harvest. Big Bud is fairly short with a traditional indica leaf structure, but unlike the stereotypical indica, can become tall and lanky if not closely tended. As with the typical indica/sativa hybrid, Big Bud may triple in size from the time the light cycle is changed. Big Bud also finishes in as few as 50 days with an impressive yield. The high is mellow with a sweet and spicy flavor, a long duration and a more indica body stone.

This variety is suitable for a sea of green method or for a garden of bigger plants. While relatively flexible, Big Bud has shown some sensitivity to the typical marijuana insects and pests. Best results occur in the indoor environment, where variables are more easily controlled. Hydro gives the best yields, but Big Bud can also thrive in soil, especially in the right outdoor conditions (not the case with the Netherlands weather). She can be expected to give the grower some beautiful flowers as long as they keep a tidy garden.

 I S

 body relaxation

 sweet and spicy

 50-65 days

 SA a x BB x Skunk 18.5 (Afghani

 up to 550 g per m2

 SOG

Big Buddha Cheese
Big Buddha Seeds

In the UK cannabis scene, the Cheese has become one of those special and elusive strains whose name is almost synonymous with good weed. Its old school flavor and sublime effects have become a standout. Cheese was cloned only in the UK, so she remained a regional phenomenon. Based on the characteristics of her taste and high, it is believed that the Cheese clone originated from 1980s Skunk and Northern Lights lineages. Cheese clones passed between many breeders and growers, and as they circulated, several breeders attempted to capture this variety's special qualities in seed form.

Big Buddha crossed the Cheese with an Afghan male plant. Then he backcrossed to the Cheese mother for two years. Big Buddha Cheese is a unique fast flowering indica with enough sativa influences to make a truly classic smoke.

The plant exhibits more than one phenotype in her growth pattern, but all retain the important properties unique to the Cheese—the special dank, incense-like aroma, the smooth distinctive flavor and the easygoing, mellow high, which settles in calmly and is virtually without a ceiling.

Big Buddha Cheese is equally well suited for indoor and outdoor gardens. Plants are ready in 7-9 weeks when grown hydroponically, and may take an additional week when grown organically in soil or in coco. Although she can be grown in an SOG system, BBC is better as a multi-branch plant, as the internodes stretch out during flowering to produce magnificent, elegant, slender kush-like buds. During the last few weeks, bulging calyxes and glistening resin production appear when the plant is fully ripened.

Outdoors, BBC will finish in most parts of Europe well before the first frosts sets in, but the yield depends on the appropriateness of the climate. In the smell department, you have been warned! BBC starts to emanate a pong as early as the formation of the 7th node, cutting through most other smells, so Big Buddha advises taking steps to control odor both indoors and out.

Taste is where this variety shines. When properly dried and cured, the flavor has a special "dank" quality reminiscent of what good pot used to taste like—spicy, sweet, and kush-like. The high is very up. It can be consumed every day with little or no immunity or change in quality of the high, making BBC suitable for both recreational and medicinal use.

1st Prize, 2006 *High Times* Cannabis Cup, Best Indica category

uplifting, no ceiling, clear, long lasting

old school, woodsy fresh/pungent

49-63 days/end Oct.- beg Nov.

♀ Cheese x ♂ Afghani

300 - 450 g/m² (1½ oz/ft²)

Photo: Nadim Sabella

Who's got the Cheese!

The history of Big Buddha Seeds

By Big Buddha

There are many different stories about its origin, but the consensus is that it came from some Original Seed Bank skunk seeds planted in 1988/1989 by the Exodus collective. This group of free party people was based at "the Manor," a large old home just outside of London. Exodus was taking a lead role in fighting prohibition at that time and the Manor was a persecution-free zone. It inspired loads of people to start growing, and cuttings were flying out of the door for a few years! Due to its great taste and all-prevailing stench, one of the group decided to name this plant the Cheese.

During the late 1990s I was taking photos, writing articles and interviewing breeders for Weed World magazine in the UK, and making good contacts within the industry. Eventually I was given some cuttings from a much respected member of the UK cannabis scene, Zorro from Red Eye magazine. This was when we started our backcrossing projects. We gave out a lot of our crosses to other growers as well as selecting the right progeny for breeding. Among those strains was one we named "The Kali," a really fat spicy Afghan strain. Kali was a special line, so the male from these seedlings was chosen to start the backcrossing of the clone-only Cheese.

With the ever changing fashion for different variants and flavors of cannabis, we are constantly researching and testing to find that special plant.

53

Black Domina
Sensi Seed Bank

Black Domina is a powerful smoke. Her resinous buds range from a harsh peppery scent to the dark smell of blackberries. Not intended for the sweet tooth, Black Domina buds taste smoky and spicy, leaving some tokers wondering if the pipe contains hashish along with the weed. She embodies the indica high, with overpowering body effects. While possibly devastating if used in the wrong circumstances, this strain is a great buzz for a day off or a nightcap when no serious work lies ahead.

This multiple cross is basically the result of stacking four of Sensi's heaviest selected indicas in one hybrid: the Afghani SA, the Ortega hybrid developed in Canada, and a combination of the Hash Plant and the famed Northern Lights, both of which have origins in the U.S. Pacific Northwest. Because 4-way hybrids are hard to stabilize, expect the F1 hybrid to show some variation—but also expect 90 percent of your plants to drip with resin.

The Black Domina plant has large bracts and wide-fingered, indica-style leaves. This variety was intended for indoor cultivation, and boasts a flower finishing time of under 2 months. The sea of green method is appropriate, but Black Domina will also be good as bigger, multi-branched plants. If attempted outdoors, she may tend to run or produce lesser quality buds if the conditions are less than optimal. Growers at Sensi's Cannabis Castle recommend hydroponics for a clean and easy grow with the quickest and best results.

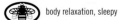 body relaxation, sleepy

 acrid, hasy, peppery

 50 days

 Afghani x Ortega 6 x Hash Plant

 up to 430 g per m²

 SOG

54

Blue Cheese
Big Buddha Seeds

Blue Cheese was created by crossing a set of Blueberry males, acquired from several different breeders, with Big Buddha Cheese, the backbone of many of Big Buddha's breeding projects (see Big Buddha Cheese). The resulting seeds were grown out and a male was selected from 40 different Blueberry x Cheese male contestants, becoming the proud papa of this pungent strain. The selected Blueberry Cheese male was then crossed once again with a Big Buddha Cheese female, making this hybrid a mostly cheese plant with a hint of blueberry.

Blue Cheese has round swirls of compact flowers that develop distinctly purple hues near the finish. The close internodes of this plant make it highly suitable for sea of green growing. Indoor plants in SOG mature in 8-10 weeks. She produces a huge main cola indoors or out, with respectable additions to the yield from the controlled side branching. In the last two weeks, this strain shows a real burst of resin and starts to deliver a truly funky smell. Outdoors, this strain finishes around Halloween.

Blue Cheese's flavor has a soft fruity kiss of blueberry that fans of the fruit will appreciate, anchored in a strong underlying flavor that is unmistakably Cheese—slightly funky and dank with a woodsy edge. The combined taste is musky and spicy with a sweet cotton candy note and a hint of berries on the exhale. While the yield is not as abundant as some commercial strains selected for their pumped-up buds, growers in search of connoisseur flavors will find the yield to be generous when compared to other varieties in this category.

The biggest pleasure of the Blue Cheese is its high, which comes on smooth and easy, and stays very functional while creating a feeling of great euphoria and an opening into the awareness of possibility, bringing with it the potential to face the day with a positive outlook. This high opens the mind by relaxing the body. It's a comforting, balanced vibe that can take a nice long walk, or sit by the fire at home.

 I S 80/20

 physical, muscle relaxation

 sweet, rose, violet, apple

 63 days/early Oct.

 ♀ Skunk/Northern Lights x ♂ El Nino

 up to 700 g/m² in; up to 1000 g/ plant out

 SOG

Photo: Gracie Malley

How Cannabis Gets You High

By William Dolphin & Chris X, PhD

The history of cannabis consumption stretches back at least four millennia, but the actual chemistry of the plant has only been unlocked in the last forty years.

The Plant Side: Cannabinoids

Marijuana is composed of over 400 compounds, including about 60 cannabinoids, which are a class of molecules unique to the cannabis plant. Cannabinoids were first identified in the 1940s, but it was not until 1964 that Dr. Raphael Mechoulam of the Hebrew University of Jerusalem isolated delta-9 tetrahydrocannabinol (THC), as the primary psychoactive ingredient in pot, the chemical that gets people high.

The molecular formula of THC is C21H30O2, with a molecular weight of 314.45 and a boiling point of 200°C (392°F).

THC's effects are modulated by the other cannabinoids. Along with THC, the main cannabinoids are cannabidiol (CBD), cannabinol (CBN) and cannabigerol (CBG). More than 50 other cannabinoids are either slight chemical variations on these main four molecules, or are only present in extremely small quantities in comparison. THC is by far the best understood.

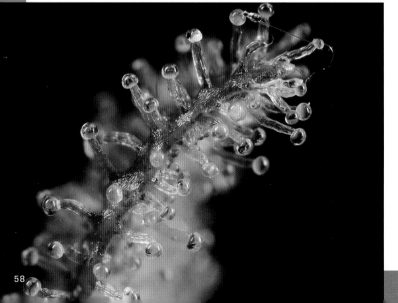

Cannabinoids are concentrated in a thick resin produced in glandular structures known as trichomes. This name comes from the Greek, and means "growth of hair." On marijuana plants, trichomes are the tiny stalks with cannabinoid-filled heads that stick up off the buds, leaves and stems. In addition to cananbinoids, trichomes are also rich in terpenes, the chemicals that produce the powerful, distinctive odors of the cannabis plant.

This close-up shows the glandular structure of marijuana resin. The ball atop the stem is the trichome. It contains the cannabinoids, responsible for the high, and the terpenes, responsible for the odor and flavor of cannabis.

Photo: Professor P from Dynasty Seeds

The Human Side: Cannabinoid Receptors

Cannabinoid receptors are found in very large quantities in many different parts of the nervous system, which includes the brain, spinal cord and the nerves that carry signals between the brain and body. Most of the cannabis high is the result of THC interacting with the cannabinoid receptors in the nervous system.

In 1988 an American research team discovered the part of the brain that picks up THC and other cannabinoids. Dubbed CB-1 receptors, they seem to be responsible for the euphoric and anticonvulsive effects of cannabis. CB-1 receptors are found in many parts of the nervous system and reproductive system, but are virtually absent from areas that control the lungs and heart. Marijuana bypasses these systems, making it essentially non-toxic. Most drugs, even aspirin or coffee, act on these vital systems, which means at high enough doses, they can be toxic or fatal to humans. On the contrary, there are no recorded deaths from a marijuana overdose. The effects of THC overconsumption are generally restricted to conditions that may include severe temporary memory impairment, paranoia and panic, but most often result in sleepiness followed by deep and sometimes prolonged sleep.

Scientists identified a second group of cannabis receptors known as CB-2 receptors. These are found in the immune system, primarily the spleen, but also in other organs. They appear to be responsible for the anti-inflammatory and stress reduction effects of marijuana. The CB-2 receptors may hold the key to many other therapeutic effects that this plant offers, such as immune modulation and tumor reduction.

Having identified these receptors, researchers naturally wondered what they were doing there in the first place. In 1992, Dr. Devane, along with a scientific team working at Dr. Mechoulam's project, was able to identify the chemical produced by the body naturally that the receptors are there to receive.

Devane named these naturally occuring chemicals "anandamides" after the Sanskrit word for bliss (ananda). Technically, they are described as "endogenous ligands." They activate the cannabinoid receptors. The effects of the natural chemicals are similar to THC, but act less powerfully and disappear far faster.

The discovery of these anandamides makes it clear that while cannabinoid receptors sure come in handy for getting high on pot, their sole purpose is not to allow humans to get high from cannabis. The cannabinoid system appears to be very ancient, and exists in nearly all species of animals so far investigated—mammals, reptiles and birds, even very simple ones like the microscopic hydra.

According to Mechoulam's ongoing research, anandamides may play a critical role in controlling many of the body's biochemical systems, including reproduction, sleep, fight-or-flight and appetite cycles. The presence of these naturally occurring "anandamides" gives new meaning to the saying "get high on life." Our bodies naturally take advantage of this feel-good chemistry for their own regulatory purposes.

Photo: Barge

The evolution of vaporizers from (clockwise from top left) a Volcano bag, to Cloud Penz, the Firefly and Pax.

The Cannabis-Human Interaction

Once THC reaches a cell, it binds to the receptor, causing changes in the cell's function, which ultimately result in the physiological or psychological effects of the drug—in other words, it makes you high.

The body absorbs pot when the cannabinoids are released and inhaled as smoke or vapor. They pass through the lining of the lungs and enter the bloodstream. Blood circulates through the heart, then heads straight for the brain and on to other parts of the body, resulting in a rapid onset of effects.

When cannabis is eaten or drunk as a beverage, the cannabinoids are not absorbed until they've made it past the stomach to the intestines, where they are absorbed into the blood, which passes through the liver before distribution to the brain and other parts of the body.

Photo: Barge

Once THC passes through the liver, it is chemically modified into 11-hydroxy-THC. Because digestion and absorption are relatively inefficient and slow, the effects are delayed for 30-60 minutes from consumption, but once they begin, they last longer.

The quality of the "high" from inhalation versus eating may be different, since most of the eaten THC will be modified by the liver. Also, only about 30% of the THC is absorbed when eaten, while 50-75% is absorbed when pot is inhaled, whether smoked or vaporized.

A scientific study of subjects smoking marijuana determined what factors affected blood levels of THC. It was discovered that longer breath holding time was more important than the number of puffs taken or the "puff volume." That's right. Roll your eyes at your smoking pals when they seem on the verge of exploding from holding an inhale—science is on their side.

Once pot reaches the receptors, it has a multitude of effects. Scientific researchers have indicated four main groups of psychological categories that make up the high[†]:

Emotional: euphoria, easy laughter, decreased anxiety
Sensory: increased or altered perception of external stimuli; increased awareness of one's own body

†Adapted from Perez-Reyes, M. "The psychologic and physiologic effects of active cannabinoids." In Nahas, G., et al, Marijuana and Medicine. Totowa, NJ; Humana Press, 1999, pp. 245-252.

Somatic: feeling of floating or sinking, impaired balance
Cognitive: distortion of time perception, memory lapses, difficulty concentrating

Physiological effects may include a brief increase in heart rate and blood pressure, red eyes, dry mouth, decreased activity of the intestines and decreased nausea, analgesia (pain relief), decreased convulsions (anti-seizure) and decreased muscle spasms. These effects may be present to greater or lesser degrees depending on the balance of cannabinoids and the amount of the dose.

The Science of Variety

Remember the two types of receptors? THC attaches primarily to CB-1 receptors, while CBD has an affinity for CB-2 receptors. Since some varieties have a larger proportion of CBD relative to THC or vice versa, this is one scientific basis for different strains producing a range of effects. More CBD typically produces a heavier, "body high," helpful with sleep or inflammation. More THC typically affects the head more, generating euphoria and energy.

Connoisseurs appreciate the subtleties of variation in the highs marijuana can impart. Now, the medical community is just beginning to identify physiologic reactions to certain strains that may benefit specific conditions. So far, it is believed that THC mediates pain and provides neuroprotection, while CBD relieves convulsion, inflammation, anxiety and nausea.

GW Pharmaceuticals, the British firm, has spent years and millions of dollars researching and developing cannabis-based medications. They have found that particular balances of these two cannabinoids produce measurably different effects in patients. For instance, THC or CBD alone do not help pain management nearly as much as an equal balance between the two.

Other cannabinoids also appear to have profound effects on physical function and health. Since 2002, cancer researchers have identified cannabinoids responsible for tumor reduction, triggering the natural cell death that keeps tumors from growing and cutting off the blood supply to tumors that have already developed.

Identifying and developing strains of marijuana that contain particular ratios of cannabinoids and other chemicals should prove to be some of the most important work of the next decade.

Blueberry
DJ Short

While Blueberry is a sativa/indica mix, it is sub-jectively considered a mostly indica cross. The name is obviously related to the flavor of the finished product, but also fits with the cool blue hues of the plant and buds, which will pale to a lavender blue in the curing and drying process.

Blueberry is a low to medium height plant of mostly indica structure, but with more branching, especially from the lower limbs. The plant grows full with wide, dark leaves and stems. Growing outdoors with organic fertilizers is optimal, as this allows Blueberry to retain the nuance of its flavors, making the quality utmost. This variety also performs well in terms of quality and quantity under many conditions, including the sea of green method.

The taste and aroma are very fruity, with the signature blueberry taste. This variety produces a notable and pleasantly euphoric experience of top quality, and the buzz lasts a long time. Blueberry smoke will not put you to sleep, but it may make you forget what you were going to do instead. Blueberry won first and second place for a number of Cannabis Culture "mini-Cups" sponsored by Marc Emery and Cannabis Culture magazine. Dutch Passion's version of Blueberry, which was derived from the original Delta 9 Collection, won first place in the 2000 High Times Cannabis Cup in the mostly indica category.

UPDATE: Dutch Passion Seed Company continues to offer seeds based on DJ Short's genetics.

 80/20

 euphoric

 berry of course

 50-60 days in mid-Oct out at 45° N

 Purple Thai & ♀Highland Thai x Afghan indica ♂

 25 g per f² with 40 wpf in; 300 g per plant out

 SOG

Bubble Cheese
Big Buddha Seeds

Big Buddha has been spreading the gospel of Cheese throughout the UK. In this mission, he finds a flock of Cheeseheads wherever he goes, and comes across many different versions or phenotypes of the Cheese variety, as well as seeing many Cheese crosses. One unique variation came from a friend who is affectionately nicknamed Mr. Cheese. Mr. Cheese provided the mother for what has become the Bubble Cheese. The mother was a cutting that crossed a UK Bubblegum strain with OG Cheese (Exodus). This mother was similar in growth and appearance to the original Cheese but had a much more pronounced bubblegum flavor. Big Buddha created a "father" from a "reversed" Hubba Bubba Kush from Amsterdam. In other words, Hubba Bubba Kush was induced to create pollen on a female plant in order to feminize this strain.

Bubble Cheese is a mostly indica hybrid that grows into a solid Kush-like indica plant—compact and dense, with dark green fat squatty leaves. Its branching is short, thick, and minimal, making it a good performer in a sea of green setup. Bubble Cheese is a moderate to heavy feeder who takes 8–10 weeks to finish. It is recommended for indoor gardens, but if outdoor weather stays above freezing through early November, count yourself among the lucky few who can cultivate a Bubble Cheese garden outdoors.

Expert growers or resourceful beginners with a green thumb will produce some pungent indica with this strain. Indoors, the Bubble Cheese can reach heights of up to 7 feet and produces only moderate yields, averaging 200 grams per plant. The buds are compact nuggets of chewing-gum bud, sticky sweet with resin. The yield can be supplemented by turning Bubble Cheese trimmings into hubbly bubbly hash goodness. The fat glands are there, waiting to be collected, and will not disappoint in quantity or quality.

Mixing bubblegum with cheese may not sound so delicious—until you remember that Cheese doesn't taste like, well, cheese. Cheese is the old-school spicy-sweet Kush. It possesses an aroma and flavor that when cured correctly brings back wistful memories of the primo tastes of yesteryear. This is Kush with some sugar sprinkled on top; sweet-tooth Kush fans will be very happy. The Bubble Cheese high comes on strong. Its sedating buzz has a down-tempo, sleepy bodily sensation. It is not a mental downer, but brings a positivity that allows one to wander pleasantly while listening to music or drift off into dreamland. As a medicinal aid, it is especially appropriate for insomnia or muscle pain.

 85/15

 sedative, sensual, stoney

 bubblegum, kush

 55–65 days

 Bubblegum x ♀Cheese x ♂reversed Hubba Bubba Kush

 200g per plant

 SOG

Buddha Haze
Big Buddha Seeds

Photos: Bud the Cheese 420

While living in Amsterdam, Big Buddha breeders managed to acquire many different clones for personal headstash. One of these was an amazing pheno of Amnesia Haze. This specific cutting was a Bubblegum phenotype that descended from two previous Cannabis Cup winners. The mother was an Amsterdam coffeeshop clone related to three great hazes: Super Silver Haze, Amnesia Haze, and G-13 Haze. Big Buddha took this haze pheno to Spain, where oops—she got knocked up with the feminized pollen of a Manga Rosa plant, a landrace strain acquired by friends when they traveled through Brazil.

The happy accident of this cross produced a beautiful baby girl, the Buddha Haze. This is a haze treat befitting the Buddha in everyone. She has a unique taste blending mango haze with pure sativa tones in a way that is usually found only in South America. From the start, the Buddha Haze is an attractive plant with elegant sativa-slender leaves. The haze structure has loose branching and forms heavy flower tops that benefit from supports. Indoor gardeners should flower this plant soon after establishing vegetation, since haze sativas really do like to stretch out. Given the super long 10–14 week season she requires, most Buddha Haze growers will probably be gardening indoors.

Like all haze-dominant plants, the Buddha Haze requires a gardener who is devoted, attentive, and knowledgeable. This pretty gal is a fussy plant who has particular tastes. The more experienced sativa or haze gardener will fare better with this variety. Buddha Haze eats light and does not like too many nutrients. She will cooperate in both hydro and soil systems and prefers things warmer, thriving in slightly hot environments and showing her displeasure when the room gets too chilly.

Buddha Haze's light green calyxes form compact bunches along the branches, growing long tendrils that turn copper as they mature. The smell of haze is strong in the garden air. This is one of the sweeter tasting hazes out there, mixing the pungent sweet fruit flavors with a mango edge and a hint of sweet bubblegum candy. The Buddha Haze high has no ceiling—the sky is the limit. The strong and seamless beginning builds in a long euphoric rush, making Buddha Haze good for parties or festivities of all kinds. The buzz creates a very functional state because it keeps an alert, electric, and cheerful vibe that inspires thought without causing one's mind to wander off.

 85/15

 hazy, trippy, giggly, happy

 candy, mango, fruity, haze

 75–90 days

 ♀Amnesia Haze x ♂Manga Rosa

 100g per plant

California Indica
Sensi Seed Bank

California Indica's mother was chosen from the original true-breeding Afghani lines from Sensi Seeds. After years of selective breeding, Home was selected as the mother. Home is very much like California Sweet Orange bud, but the flowers aren't as dense. By hybridizing with two heavy indica strains, the resulting California Indica produced sweet, pungent heavy buds with lots of resin.

California Indica has less foliage than most Sensi varieties, with a nice flower structure that is open and airy. The bud's hairs will turn orange upon drying. The buzz is a pleasant body relaxer with mellow effects that won't lock you on the couch after one toke. With a sweet yet pungent aroma and mostly sweet flavor, California Indica is the least "green" and the most "orange" strain that Sensi offers.

California Indica gives the best yields in the shortest time in a hydro culture garden. This plant can be grown in the sea of green style, but performs optimally when allowed to develop multiple branches. Remember that light and space are equally important in determining yield. Changes to these conditions change the yield by as much as 125 g per m2. While only appropriate for some outdoor climates, this strain has performed admirably in Spain and other dry Mediterranean type climates. Even indoors, you are best advised to keep your room a little on the dry side to avoid mold with this variety. Despite this, California Indica is a tolerant, versatile plant which performs well under many conditions.

I

 stoney

 fruity/acrid

 45-50 days in early Oct out or greenhouse

 Home and Hash Plant x Northern Lights #1 hybrid

 450 g per m2 in 500 g per plant out

The Cannabinoids

THC:

Delta-9-tetrahydrocannabinol & delta-8-tetrahydrocannabinol—THC mimics the action of anandamide, a neurotransmitter naturally produced in the body, which binds with the cannabinoid receptors in the brain to produce the "high" associated with marijuana.

THCV:

Tetrahydrocannabivarin—prevalent in certain South African and Southeast Asian strains of cannabis. Although THCV may possess many of the therapeutic properties of THC, it does not contribute significantly to marijuana's potency.

CBD:

Cannabidiol—previously believed to be psychoactive, or to contribute to the high by interacting with other cannabinoids. The most recent research indicates that CBD has a negligible effect on the high. It is however a strong anti-inflammatory, and may take the edge off some THC effects, such as anxiety. Although a non-psychoactive cannabinoid, CBD appears to be helpful for many medical conditions.

CBN:

Cannabinol—a degradation product of THC, CBN is not psychoactive, but is believed to produce a depressant effect or "fuzzy" forehead when it is present in significant quantities.

CBC:

Cannabichromene—this cannabinoid is a non-psychoactive precursor to THC.

CBG:

Cannabigerol—a non-psychoactive cannabinoid. Hemp strains often possess elevated levels of CBG while possessing only trace amounts of THC.

Cheesus
Big Buddha Seeds

When Buddha and Godbud mix it up with the Cheese, it seems only fitting that their progeny would be none other than Cheesus. This strain was developed by young bloods in the Amsterdam breeding scene. The Big Buddha Cheese female is crossed to a male Godbud from British Columbia, courtesy of the BC Bud Depot. In order to feminize the strain, the resulting hybrid was crossed with a reversed Cheesus father to render all seeds feminine.

Cheesus brings indica and sativa together in a hybrid that blends their qualities peacefully. She grows in a slender indica profile and quickly forms a structure that is solid enough to support fat colas. The leaves are a deep healthy green with a chunky indica shape. Cheesus plants do well in a sea of green or in systems that maintain multiple branches. Any growing medium is agreeable, and moderate to heavy feeding is recommended. From the thick green of this plant emerge conical buds that are dense, bringing good yields to those who are attentive, loving, and persistent. Growing Cheesus requires patience, with a lengthy flowering time of 9–12 weeks, but the results may turn you into a believer. Actually, Cheesus serves either the expert or the beginning gardener well, from any creed to none, breeding enjoyment and respect for the plant.

Few growers have the luxury to garden Cheesus outdoors, but those who do can expect to harvest around the end of October. Maximum outdoor sizes average 6–7 feet (2 meters) and deliver per-plant yields of up to 1000 grams for those who wait out the long season.

The Cheesus makes elevating head stash. It is good for everyday use, bringing on a positive and meditative enjoyment. It may encourage a talkative mood, and is not desirable for highly focused work. The flavors are deep and dank: imagine a sweet earthy incense infused with lavender and an edge of tart honey fruitiness and a little pine and spice. Cheesus has many disciples but makes no exclusive claims on your devotions. She doesn't have to—the connoisseur experience speaks for itself.

 60/40

 uplifting, talkative, euphoric

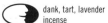 dank, tart, lavender incense

 65–80 days

 Big Buddha Cheese x ♀ BC Godbud X ♂ reversed/selfed Cheesus

 200g per plant in 1000g per plant out

The Mystery of the Seed

Ed Rosenthal

Marijuana is probably the world's most anthropomorphized plant. There are many reasons for comparisons of marijuana with human qualities. First, marijuana is an annual that completes its life cycle, from seed to plant to seed again, in a few months. You could say that every two days or so in the life of a marijuana plant is equal to a year of human life. Second, unlike all other annuals, cannabis is dioecious, plants are either male or female. Third, the sexes are dimorphic: their life cycles are somewhat different and their appearances diverge as they age.

Cultivation techniques also push us to think of marijuana somewhat differently from any other domesticated plant. Almost all other harvests, such as fruits and grains, are the bounty of fertilized flowers. However, marijuana harvests are best when the plant is kept from reproducing. To prevent this pollination, we treat the plant more like a member of the family than a farm crop. We limit her contact with the opposite sex and prevent sexual relations. The goal: virgin buds unspoiled by pollen.

We share an emotional tie with marijuana because of its ability to affect us subjectively. As a result, we sometimes think of the plants themselves as individuals, even naming them. Such names often denote our individual experiences or the sexuality of the plant.

As with humans, the reproductively ready female form of cannabis is the most desired, or at least most depicted and venerated in imagery. In most other mammals, as well as fish, birds, and reptiles, the male Is usually on exhibition.

Our familiarity and symbiotic relationship with marijuana have made the plant seem like a friend, albeit one that can get you in a lot of trouble. Step back for just a minute and set aside your warm emotions. Take a fresh look at marijuana, and you will discover an organism from the plant kingdom that parallels our life form.

Female Flower: Look a few nodes down from the plant top where a small female flower grows.

The Plant and the Seed

Do chickens produce eggs to make more chickens? Or do eggs produce chickens to make more eggs? This may seem like a frivolous question, until it is examined more deeply. The entire life of an annual plant, from seed to expiration, is spent mostly as an embryo enclosed in a pod. As soon as the seed germinates the plant begins its quest to grow and produce more seed before it dies.

As in human reproduction, the cannabis seed or embryo is the result of a complex set of parallel processes by the male and female reproductive organs, the flowers. Male flower buds look something like pawnbroker's balls. They hang down

Hermaphrodite plant: A hermaphrodite bud. Both male and female flowers are apparent. A single hermaphrodite plant can pollinate an entire garden and should be removed before their pollen is released.

Male Flower: Full-blown male flowers as they open to reveal five creamy yellow petals

from the stem. As the five-petal white or cream colored flowers open they move to face upward, making it easy for the breeze to carry away the pollen. Each pollen grain contains two sperm cells. They are haploid, meaning each holds half a set of chromosomes.

Once it catches the wind the pollen floats until it is caught on an object. A small percentage a light on a female flower's stigma. The female flower has no petals. It consists of two stigmas topping styles that attach to the ovary. A single ovule (think egg) also contains a haploid number of chromosomes.

Longitudinal Section of a Seed

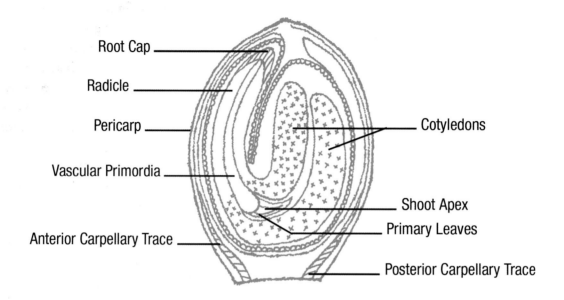

Root Cap

Radicle

Pericarp

Vascular Primordia

Anterior Carpellary Trace

Cotyledons

Shoot Apex

Primary Leaves

Posterior Carpellary Trace

When a pollen grain lands on a virgin stigma it is hydrated by a sugary liquid provided by its host. Once germinated, it grows a pollen tube that follows a path through the style to the ovary, where the single ovule is attached to the placenta at the base of the ovary's inner wall. The two sperm travel down the tube. One of them combines with the ovule to form the embryo. The other sperm combines with several eggs that have been modified in development, become infertile and gathered high-energy food and tissue that lines the ovary called "endosperm." The embryo grows as it receives nourishment from the plant through the placenta and it incorporates some of the endosperm. The rest is used for nourishment during germination.

The pericarp, the seed coat, which has developed from the ovary's outer wall, begins to harden as the seed matures and breaks away from the placenta, which dries up. The seed is now mature.

Encased inside its hard shell, the embryo is in a state of near suspended animation. It can remain viable frozen for years and can survive heat spells as well. It is activated when the outer case is hydrated in warm temperatures, above 50° F (1O° C). Within minutes of being moistened, the seed prepares for germination, which becomes visible as the tap root breaks the hard shell and emerges a few days later.

Seeds ready for germination.

We may think that our brains make the important decisions of our lives, but for the most part they have been made for us, hardwired in genetic codes. For all our efforts, our consciousness cannot alter our path through life—fetus, infant, toddler, child, adolescent, adult, geriatric, dead. Our growth and reproductive patterns are conveyer belts that never stop. Luckily, our brains don't have much to say about how-to grow teeth, where to place our eyes or how our digestive system works, because to the extent that it is able to interfere, it usually messes up. And so it is with plants—they are pre-programmed to respond to environmental conditions in ways that echo what their progenitors experienced for the past millions of years. When you think about it, we are no better adapted to the environment than cannabis. We are all survivors. The rest are called extinct.

Germination begins when the root emerges from the seed.

You can see the pericap of the seed still on top of the embryonic leaf, the cotyledon. The first true leaves are visible above the cotyledon.
Photo: John Alexander

77

Chiesel
Big Buddha Seeds

The Chiesel project started in 2006 when friend and master breeder Soma gifted Big Buddha some of his legendary New York City Diesel in seed form. Out of these seeds Big Buddha and his team selected a really nice phenotype of the diesel male to cross with the original Cheese clone.

These seeds were then given to growers in the UK, the Netherlands, and Spain to try out and report on. After the seeds were grown out, the search for a special Chiesel clone began. Big Buddha's breeding mission was to select the one with the most grapefruit-fuel taste. This Chiesel was feminized by reversing it with itself. In November 2008, Chiesel was released.

Chiesel grows like its Cheese mama—a slender but open sativa structure with indica-style leaves. It has hybrid vigor, thriving best when left with many branches and fed generously with nutrients. The buds are like pine cones—compact, oblong, and

dense with light electric green coloring and faint orange hairs. Flowering takes about 9 to 10 weeks depending on preferences and conditions. Earlier harvests will yield a taste that leans towards the Cheese/kush profile. When plants are left to flower longer, flavors are a deeper, more grapefruit kush.

Chiesel is smelly and pungent while growing. It brings the old school sublimeness that the Cheese captures together in harmony with the grapefruit fuel kush of the Diesel. The flavors of this weed can serve as a party icebreaker, getting people talking, or circling for a taste of the hashy fuel pungency with a grapefruit sour edge. With Chiesel, the party doesn't end there—this is a very up, energetic pot that has an electric enlivening feel to it. It can lead to giggling and improvisational creativity, and it has enough body balance to bring out a sensual mood when the party is only for two.

Photo: Nadim Sabella

 60/40

 uplifting, electric

 fuel, grapefruit, Thai stick

 60–75 days

 UK Cheese x New York City Diesel

 400g per plant in 1200g per plant out

 SOG

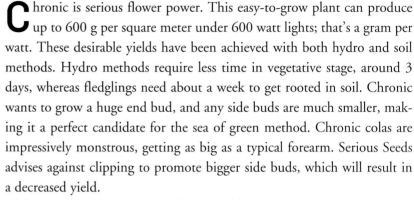

Chronic

Serious Seeds

 50/50

 even body-head

 floral

 60-67 days

 Northern Lights, Skunk x Northern Lights, AK-47

 400-600 g per m²

 SOG

Chronic is serious flower power. This easy-to-grow plant can produce up to 600 g per square meter under 600 watt lights; that's a gram per watt. These desirable yields have been achieved with both hydro and soil methods. Hydro methods require less time in vegetative stage, around 3 days, whereas fledglings need about a week to get rooted in soil. Chronic wants to grow a huge end bud, and any side buds are much smaller, making it a perfect candidate for the sea of green method. Chronic colas are impressively monstrous, getting as big as a typical forearm. Serious Seeds advises against clipping to promote bigger side buds, which will result in a decreased yield.

This once predominantly indica breed has been updated with a sativa cross and stabilizing since 2000, which improved both the strength and resin content, while leaving the subtle sweet-spicy scent intact. The high has a full spectrum of effects that typically start in the mind and then move to the body. This variety has a light wildflower scent and flavor with almost no trace of pungency or tang. The smell is subtle when the plant is alive and can be enhanced to a delicious sweetness if cured and dried properly.

Chronic has shown two phenotypes in the past. Plants have typically been either short with chubby buds or thinner with more elongated, slightly fluffed buds on taller plants. Since the breeding work at the start of the new century, Chronic has become more uniform, resembling the latter, more elongated type. The buds are also denser and more resinous than before. Chronic flowers early, and shows gender easily, with good sized preflowers at the base of the fan leaves along the stem. This variety won 3rd place in the 1994 *High Times* Cannabis Cup in the hydro division.

Simon on the Chronic:

"**A**long with AK-47 and the original Kali Mist, Chronic was bred in the days when Serious still had an enormous space to conduct experiments: the early 1990s. Chronic was first developed in 1994 with the goal of producing a plant that combined quality with a good yield. Up until that point, it seemed like there was some discrepancy between these two selection characteristics, and growers often had to sacrifice one for the other. I wanted to create a variety that proved this idea wrong, something that produced enormous buds without compromising a quality high for an enjoyable flavor or vice versa.

After its introduction, Chronic won 3rd place in the *High Times* Cannabis Cup in the hydro division—that was the only time it was entered in the Cup. But many other power-hitting indica strains have been released since 1994 that follow along the same lines, offering up both quality and yield with a mostly indica stone. By the late 1990s, Chronic seemed 'dated.' I decided it was time to give it a little more complexity and refresh this variety without losing any of the characteristics that made it so well-liked to start out with. I bred more sativa into the indica-dominant Chronic, which gave it a more complex, full-spectrum high without losing the nice yield and flavor. The facelift also improved both the strength and resin content.

The mildly sweet scent with a bit of spiciness also stayed intact, but curing and drying are fundamental to carrying this characteristic from the live plant to the smokeable product. Even while living, the wildflower scent is subtle, but it will be lost for good if not dried properly. When put in plastic before completely dry, the scent is irreversibly gone, more so for this variety than for any others I've worked with. But if you let it dry thoroughly, the aroma develops a very strong, sweet smell which doesn't fade. This could be the difference between thinking Chronic is okay or fabulous pot for flavor connoisseurs."

Double Dutch
Magus Genetics

Photo: Green Born Identity

Double Dutch mixes the genetics of the Warlock male with a pre-2000 Chronic female, two popular native Dutch varieties. The Warlock—Magus Genetics' foundation strain—is a branchy plant with a pleasurable scent. Chronic, a strain developed by Serious Seeds in the 1990s, forms massive colas. Their offspring, Double Dutch, shows its indica pedigree by developing fat leaves, thick stems, and a bushy growth pattern during its seedling and vegetative stages. In the flowering stage, this variety produces giant sativa-like buds similar to elongated popcorn balls.

Bred for indoor gardens, Double Dutch performs well in bio, coco and hydro growth mediums, but hydro is recommended if yield is the main objective. Large gardens allow multi-branching, but staking is necessary due to Double Dutch's willowy branches and weighty flowers. However, when a relatively small number of plants are grown, the growth pattern tends to be shorter and much less lateral. Therefore, sea of green is possible with a smaller garden, but is still not the most productive setup.

Most taste buds will appreciate the pleasant fruity wildflower flavor that is also apparent in the scent. The buzz is complex and strong with both cerebral and bodily components. It starts in the mind and slowly flows down the torso into a more body-centered buzz that is lazy, but not sleepy. This buzz allows one to drift in its sensation for 2-4 hours depending on tolerance level.

 60/40

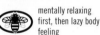 mentally relaxing first, then lazy body feeling

 wildflower/fruit

 55-65 days

 ♀ Chronic (pre-2000) x ♂ Warlock

 350-600 g/m² (1-2 oz./ft.²)

Dr. Grinspoon
Barney's Farm

This unusual pure sativa heirloom strain has been named in honor of physician, Harvard professor, author, and cannabis advocate Dr. Lester Grinspoon. By Dr. Grinspoon's own account, he first researched cannabis in order to document its harmfulness. Instead, as he reviewed the literature, he found little support for the demonization of marijuana, and much more support for its benign, positive influences. As a good scientist, Dr. Grinspoon adjusted his opinion based on the evidence. In 1971, he wrote a seminal book, Marihuana Reconsidered, which argued for the legalization of marijuana. Since that time, Grinspoon has been a steadfast and outspoken advocate, using his voice to help reform marijuana policies in the US and around the world.

The aptly named Dr. Grinspoon variety is a "thinking man's" sativa of the highest order. This top-shelf connoisseur breed is a good addition to personal gardens seeking premium headstash. The plant has a distinct flowering pattern that makes it a standout in the garden. The pure sativa heritage means Dr. Grinspoon forms long twig-like branches with the buds loosely strung popcorn-style along the willowy stems. As the plants mature, they begin to fill gaps between bud sites, but the buds remain distinct rather than gathering into one large flower. Yields are moderate with harvests up to 350 grams per square meter. Yields are likely to be better under the tutelage of a gardener who has already grown a few crops and figured out the basics.

The long season makes this an indoor or greenhouse variety when living outside of the equatorial region. Outdoors, Dr. Grinspoon needs 6 full months of agreeable weather to finish, ripening in late October or early November. Using organic fertilizers in soil will bring out the best flavors. The Dr. Grinspoon variety tends to interest gardeners with some experience and a desire for great sativa qualities. It is not "fast-food" style weed for those wanting a quick crop. This is more like a bottle of good champagne. Although Dr. Grinspoon has an effervescent lucidity that makes it suitable for any occasion, these buds are often treasured and reserved to celebrate special moments.

The aroma has the tropical-floral elements expected of an island sativa, but there is also a distinct lemon-herbal sumac smell. These notes are carried through in the flavor, imparting a light lemon tang and a touch of honeyed earthiness. This strain's clarity will be manna for the true aficionado. Dr. Grinspoon has a pleasant entry into the high, inviting a blissful and expansive mood that enhances compassion and provokes intellectual insights. It is very compatible as a daytime smoke or for long evenings with friends, intimate conversations, and deep enjoyment. Given the heightened awareness it encourages, it is less suitable right before retiring for sleep. The effects of Dr. Grinspoon taper off gradually, leaving one as clearheaded at finish as they were at the outset, only quite possibly with a host of new ideas and pleasant experiences to remember.

 electric, euphoric

 honey, earthy

 100 days

 ♀sativa x ♂sativa

 50g per plant in 200g per plant out

 in preferred

Dr. Grinspoon –
A Champion for Legalization

"One day, I hope, we will look back and wonder why our societies were so perverse as to treat cannabis as they did for the greater part of the twentieth century."
—*Dr. Lester Grinspoon*

Dr. Grinspoon's first foray into the world of cannabis began with a research project nearly 40 years ago. At the time, Lester Grinspoon was an associate professor of psychiatry at Harvard Medical School. It was the end of the 1960s, and the exponential rise of marijuana use among American youth concerned him. He was sure that young people, oblivious to the dangers, were smoking cannabis to their own detriment, and given his background as a medical doctor and academic researcher, he approached it in the way one might expect—by studying the problem. However, the more he reviewed the scientific and medical literature, the less he found to support his position. As a reputable scientist, Dr. Grinspoon kept an open mind and, rather than clinging rigidly to his initial view, he was compelled by the evidence to reverse his opinion and acknowledge marijuana's beneficence. This change of position from marijuana as menace to marijuana as harmless was the basis for his 1971 book *Marihuana Reconsidered*.

Back in the 1970s, Dr. Grinspoon had optimistically believed that the laws would change within the decade. It seemed obvious that the evidence and the laws were in contradiction. The only rational thing to do would be to change the law to reflect the reality. As we all know, when it comes to marijuana, rational policy has been a rare commodity.

Of course, since the 1970s, much new research bolsters Dr. Grinspoon's position. Since that time, Dr. Grinspoon has continued to use his considerable skills to advocate for legalization, publicly speaking and writing on the merits of cannabis, and serving as a public voice to help counteract the damaging misinformation on this plant. He has served as an expert witness in dozens of trials, and testified before Congress. He continues to insist that marijuana's most dangerous aspect is its criminalized status. Dr. Grinspoon's impeccable credentials and impressive position at Harvard have lent great credibility to claims of marijuana's safety. It took much bravery and integrity to go against society's views.

Finally, in the last decade, the work and bravery of many activists has started a wave of change in the law, although there is still more to be done. Correcting the misinformation about marijuana has required prolonged effort, and we are thankful to Dr. Grinspoon for bringing his intelligence, eloquence, and good humor to righting this wrong. It is the work of pioneers such as Lester Grinspoon that has led the way to greater sanity in our treatment of this amazingly diverse plant.

Dutchmen's Royal Orange
Flying Dutchmen

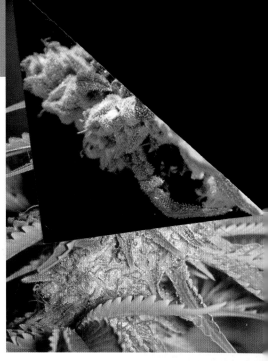

Dutchmen's Royal Orange has an international heritage. The Skunk #1 father was a stable hybrid of a Mexican/Colombian mother bred with a pure Afghan strain father. Royal Orange's indica mother, California Orange, originally came from Afghanistan by way of California. These parents were brought together by a legendary breeder in Holland in 1985.

This regal variety has a delectably sweet smell combined with a hashish taste exposing the Afghani mother's influence. The Royal Orange buzz is a strongly physical sensation good for kicking back in the sun, or on the couch for a long epic movie. Even with the strong bodily sensation, this variety retains the clear high of the Skunk parent.

Dutchmen's Royal Orange leaves are shiny and dark, with a typical indica plant structure overall—relatively short and wide with broad leaves. The buds are tight rocky nuggets, which along with the minimal vegetation makes this a high yielder. Despite this density, Royal Orange has terrific mold resistance and is very uniform in its growth habits, making it ideal for greenhouse cultivation. Flying Dutchmen recommends growing in soil using organic methods for best results.

body relaxation/ clear head

very sweet citrus

63–77 days in Oct out

♂Skunk #1 x ♀California Orange

up to 500 g per m²

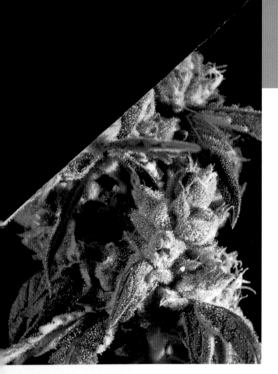

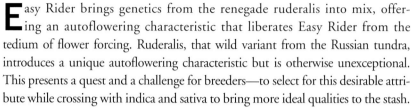

Easy Rider brings genetics from the renegade ruderalis into mix, offering an autoflowering characteristic that liberates Easy Rider from the tedium of flower forcing. Ruderalis, that wild variant from the Russian tundra, introduces a unique autoflowering characteristic but is otherwise unexceptional. This presents a quest and a challenge for breeders—to select for this desirable attribute while crossing with indica and sativa to bring more ideal qualities to the stash.

Ceres undertook this quest by crossing ruderalis to a Dutch indica-dominant strain from the skunk line well-known for its classical taste and high as well as its versatility in breeding. The result is a short, compact autoflowering plant that can grow successfully in conditions that would otherwise seem impossible: high in the mountains, high up in northern latitudes, or in conditions with lousy lighting or light pollution that would make a 12-hour dark cycle unfeasible. Since it is a cross, there is a chance that one or two plants will be indica-dominant, lacking the ruderalis autoflowering trait and waiting for the light cycle to flower.

The compactness of the Easy Rider plant make it suitable for small spaces and growing the plants close together, giving each about 6 square inches of space. Each plant only yields about a half-ounce, but yields are often still substantial due to the number of plants that can fit in a small garden. Easy Rider looks like a dwarf indica, with thick jade-colored leaves and small but solid buds. This is a 'bud on a stick' plant, surrounded by a lion's crest of minimal foliage so that sea of green gardening is a natural choice, and manicuring is a breeze. At finish, this plant is only about 2 feet (60 cm), which is a nice stealth quality. This modest plant can hide below a picket fence, banister, or balcony ledge. To add to its clandestine qualities, Easy Rider can be planted very early in the year and finish when other varieties are barely halfway through their growth cycle. The short season allows Easy Rider to serve as stash while the rest of the garden grows. Its sturdiness in colder temps also make it a good second crop, because it beats the rain in temperate climates and finishes before mold or bugs can settle in. An entire cycle can be completed start to finish in 60 days.

At finish, Easy Rider gets dark green, and the hairs turn a burnished copper-brown. Easy Rider is low on smell, both when growing and even when drying or being handled. The quality of the smell will depend on whether it was grown indoors or out, but its modest smell is a pungent, slightly acrid indica odor. This follows through in the flavor with an earthy depth and sour acerbic bite. The front flavor will cause a slight mouthwatering effect. Easy Rider's flavor is decent, but not remarkable. The high is a clear headed indica body stone. It does not induce the sleepy eye-droop look, but it is better suited as a sleeping aid than a party favor.

 body stone

 acrid, earthy

 45 days

 ♀Dutch indica x ♂ruderalis

 14g per plant

 SOG

Ed Rosenthal Super Bud

Sensi Seed Bank

 65/35

 creative, light-hearted

 tropical, fruit salad

 55-65 days/Nov. 1

 Afghanis, North Indian, Thai, African, Mexican, Jamaican

 up to 500g/m² in; up to 135g/plant in/ up to 500g/plant out

 SOG

Sensi Seed Bank has released this elite strain in honor of Ed Rosenthal, the undisputed heavyweight champion of growing gurus. Literally decades in the making, this hybrid achieves a superb layering of traits from both the indica and sativa ends of the cannabis spectrum. This variety was refined from the "Potent Evolved Hybrid" project, where pure Afghani cultivars and equatorial sativa strains were interbred over many years, and their offspring selected for potency and yield at every step. The blend of tropical genes in ER Super Bud's background is especially wide-ranging, representing sativas from all around the equatorial zone—Africa, South East Asia, Central America and the Caribbean.

Ed Rosenthal Super Bud thrives outdoors in hot climates, and should be grown indoors in temperate or cold regions like Holland. Any medium is fine, and plants enjoy standard to generous fertilizer feedings. ER Super Bud is very manageable as she grows, with a surprisingly uniform growth pattern given her diverse heritage. This strain is suitable for sea of green; alternatively, both her indica and sativa phenotypes can be grown into excellent multi-stem plants.

Succulent flower formation is the Super Bud strain's distinguishing feature. All females exhibit flower structures bursting with indica density, made even fatter by the running sativa tendency. The result is buds that swell upwards and outwards to crazy sizes and sport a stupendous covering of full-sized resin glands. ER buds also have a unique pistil formation—the oversized antennae sprouting from each calyx are covered with a visible fuzz of tiny hairs, giving them a 'woolly' appearance. Different individuals show extra sativa or indica influence through subtle variations in the development and structure of their resin-soaked buds. The sativa-leaning females make particularly good multi-stem plants and produce huge oval calyxes which spiral into crooked bud-pyramids large enough to bend branches.

The indica phenotype's flowers are distinct and impressive, building into voluptuous columns of snowy bud with main colas as thick as an arm. In other respects, phenotype variation is small, with a majority of plants flowering at the same speed and increasing their height by about 150%. A small proportion will show a jump at the onset of blooming, which first widens the gaps between internodes and later gives an even greater yield potential.

All plants from this strain are sweet smelling and taste of pineapple punch. As for the stone—get ready for an immediate body flush, a bright physical glow that's not given to lethargy. Later, a cerebral high creeps up, subtle at first, yet longer lasting than the body effect. Ed Rosenthal Super Bud is sweetly relaxing, leaving plenty of energy for conversation and socializing with friends. Medicinally, this might be a good variety for chronic body pain and the blues that come with it.

Ed Rosenthal Super Bud

Sensi Seed Bank

From the inception of the modern cannabis revolution, Ed Rosenthal has been at the heart of the movement, a committed and fearless campaigner for truth, justice and sanity, which is to say, an end to prohibition.

If you've ever grown ganja, it's a safe bet that Ed has helped you out in a big way, whether directly or indirectly. He's taught generations of growers about the science and art of cannabis cultivation, and helped them discover their green thumb as well as the joys and potential for personal enrichment that this hobby can awaken.

As the brain behind the Ask Ed columns in Cannabis Culture and High Times, and the author of a veritable library of cannabis books that cover every topic from growing to law reform, Ed Rosenthal has done more than anyone we know to spread accurate, no-nonsense information on the world's most delightful crop.

It's no exaggeration to say that Ed Rosenthal Super Bud has been decades in the making. Sharp-eyed cannabis historians and collectors of old seed catalogues might have seen the single printed reference to the breeding

program that eventually led to the Super Bud strain. In 1989, this Ed-affiliated strain was called Ed's Potent Evolved Hybrid Type 1 (PEHT), when it was briefly offered in a limited edition of 1500 seeds. It sold out very quickly and was never commercially offered again. Around this time, there was a big shift toward indoor cultivation and few growers had the time or space for experimental crossings. Sensi Seed Bank's releases in the following years were geared toward this new indoor trend, featuring stabilized F1 hybrids—strains that could be relied upon for predictable behavior.

As the years passed, and Sensi's breeding-stock expanded into a truly comprehensive collection of traditional cultivars and legendary hybrids, their breeders found plenty of fascinating new possibili-

ties to explore, and the PEHT program continued quietly in the background. With occasional infusions of promising new genetic material and dozens more generations of crossing and selection for yield and resin production, the program yielded several rarefied plants which proved to be valuable intermediate parents in complex hybrids.

A desirably heavy, sticky form began to dominate the later PEHT generations. Breeders focused on stabilizing the finer points of the emerging strain. Unique flower structures and flavors discovered in the program were successfully reproduced as recurring traits and the ER seed strain neared completion. By this time, near the end of the 1990s, Holland's tolerance for cannabis was in sharp decline, and professional breeding became much more difficult, as the large crops of test seedlings required for rigorous selection were no longer possible.

As a result, the small amount of refinement required before releasing ER in its final distinct form took many years longer than expected, making this hybrid the longest single project in the Sensi Seed Bank collection. Sensi feels this world-class strain shows the years of work and care invested in its development. This gourmet hybrid promises to be a special addition to any serious aficionado's garden.

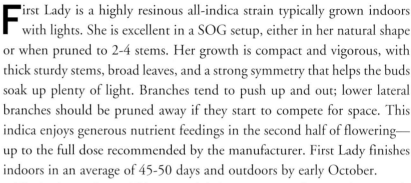

First Lady

Sensi Seed Bank

100% indica

mellow, relaxing

spicy/earthy

45-50 days/early Oct.

♀Afghani T x
♂ Ortega

up to 100 g/plant

below 45° N latitude

First Lady is a highly resinous all-indica strain typically grown indoors with lights. She is excellent in a SOG setup, either in her natural shape or when pruned to 2-4 stems. Her growth is compact and vigorous, with thick sturdy stems, broad leaves, and a strong symmetry that helps the buds soak up plenty of light. Branches tend to push up and out; lower lateral branches should be pruned away if they start to compete for space. This indica enjoys generous nutrient feedings in the second half of flowering—up to the full dose recommended by the manufacturer. First Lady finishes indoors in an average of 45-50 days and outdoors by early October.

The buds are classic Afghani—solid clusters at every bract and internode that form tight round nuggets crowning a collar of fat, dark green leaves. Plants exposed to cool breezes have a tendency to develop purple tones in the calyxes and even more pronounced in the foliage. Calyxes at the apex of terminal buds may start to build on top of each other after the lower part of the plant is mature, leading to multi-peaked tops. The most weight is produced on the unpruned main stem or on topped stems that have been properly vegetated.

The overall shape of the plant is more spruce than conifer; it has a central column of bud as its main feature rather than a more umbrella-like canopy. Like many indicas, the First Lady increases 50-100% from its vegetative height during flowering. Its size is manageable in an indoor setup, and can be controlled in a range from a minimal 1¼ feet (40 cm) to a max 4.3 feet (130 cm) when vegged for 4-6 weeks. When allowed to vegetate to a larger size, this plant averages 100 grams per plant indoors.

First Lady is a naturally tough robust plant with a healthy resilience to pests or other inhospitable garden conditions. This robustness combined with the fast finish makes it satisfying for beginners. If irrigated well, she can withstand heat, and stress from fluctuations in temperature from day to night; however, this Afghani native appreciates a dry atmosphere, especially in the later part of flowering. The easiest mistake with this variety might be overwatering or creating an overly humid atmosphere. First Lady's resilient genetics make her a good candidate for cloning.

First Lady's flavor is spicy with some acridity and earthiness, and a gentle honey undertone. The immediate stoney hit segues into a long lasting body-centered buzz. This warm, happy high encourages an affinity and contentment with one's surroundings and can greatly enhance sensual pleasures, whether they be food, music or physical contact. While functional, this high is better for lounging on a weekend than motivating oneself to get up and out. It is a good appetite stimulator and muscle relaxer and might be good for a camping weekend.

First Lady

When seeds of exotic, stocky, hash-making strains from Afghanistan, Pakistan and northern India were first introduced to the west a generation ago, they changed the face of indoor growing and made names like Kandahar and Mazar-i-Sharif part of the cannabis lexicon. Many growers are interested in strains that preserve the original Indica characteristics, before they were mixed with today's diverse, global cannabis gene-pool. So there's always a good reason to release a back-to-basics Afghani. The challenge was to release one that could stand alongside Afghani #1 and Maple Leaf Indica. First Lady exemplifies the qualities of the original Indica females whose genes are now carried in hundreds of hybrid strains. Also, when flowered alongside other strains, these Afghani girls should be the first of your ladies to finish.

Flo
DJ Short

A member of DJ Short's Delta 9 Blue Collection, Flo is an exciting plant. A sativa look-alike that matures early, Flo's name may reflect this plant's unique ability to produce a continual flow of buds through multiple harvesting.

Flo's large, tight, spear-shaped buds are made up of small, densely-packed, purple-striped calyxes. A very productive, fast maturing plant, Flo gets tall, and likes to branch out. The first buds are ripe by the end of September at or near the 45 parallel North. About every 10 to 12 days after reaching initial maturity, new buds form and can be harvested through the end of November, or as long as the plant can remain alive in the given outdoor conditions. Indoors, buds mature by the end of the 6th week of 12/12 light and are still producing mature buds into the 7th week. If you harvest only once, the yield will be more modest. Due to the Flo's multi-harvest potential, it is ideal for greenhouse production.

Flo has an energetic, motivating buzz with unusual clarity. This is true wake and bake pot, great to start the day off right without losing sight of your intentions. The flavor has a floral quality similar to Nepalese Temple Hash, with a touch of the blueberry tones that remind you they are relatives. The smell echoes the taste, remaining subtle and light. Flo was rated #1 at the 1996 Cannabis Cup by Cannabis Culture magazine.

 60/40

 active, cerebral

 floral

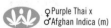 42-49 days in end Sep out at 45° N

 ♀Purple Thai x ♂Afghan Indica (m)

 25 g per f² with 40 wpf 500 g per plant out

Fruit of the Gods
Delta 9 Labs

Terpenes: Th Chemistry Odors

Ed Rose

Boo

Many cannabis fans may feel that marijuana is ambrosia for the mind and soul, a gift from above for weary mortals. The type of weed that creates such gratitude and adulation is certainly a part of Delta-9's breeding goals. Their strain Fruit of the Gods is sativa-dominant hybrid with a narrow profile and a satisfying yield. This variety's effect can be summed up in a word—uplifting! The nickname "FOG" also evolved from the thick white fog of sweet exhale after a big bong hit of this bud.

When grown indoors in a controllable flowering environment, Fruit of the Gods takes 9½ to 11 weeks to finish, depending on whether she is grown in soil or using hydro methods. This variety can also be grown outdoors in many regions. Warmer outdoor climates will result in yields that are 25-50% higher than indoor or temperate grows. Delta-9 uses neem oil for pest control with this strain, although FOG is naturally quite bug-resistant, and resilient under many growing conditions.

When Delta-9 grows out their strains, they use soil exclusively, with organic nutrients. However, FOG will do well in any indoor system, and may even be more prodigious and ripen in slightly less time with a hydroponic setup. While her height will depend on the length of the vegetative period, FOG is a moderate grower. She starts stretching out a bit in the first two weeks of flowering, and doubles in height by week three. These plants create many long side branches that hug the main stem. Her leaves are short and wide, like the leaves on her Skunk #1 poppa. They are narrower than a typical sativa leaf, so the end result is a broad elongated leaf blade. Overall, FOG looks like a small bushy plant with many branches close to the main stem. Even when kept short and grown in small spaces, Fruit Of the Gods produces well: in an average-sized room with proper ventilation and lighting, FOG will give you a minimum of 30-50 grams per 3 ft. (1 m) plant.

The "fruits" of this strain are light and airy as they fill in during the first 5 to 8 weeks. Then in the last 3 weeks they harden. Their calyxes swell up and become tight, creating small but very dense buds. FOG tastes sweet, with a hazy, floral perfume that lingers throughout the room in the thick white cloud of its exhale. The FOG high is clear-headed and uplifting. As such it is very functional and easy to maintain even during a period of work or socializing. As soon as the buzz reaches your head, it creates a momentum to get things done, and motivate with friends or focus on a project.

 mostly sativa

 uplifting

 fruity, floral

 66-77 days

 Northern Lights 5 Haze (mother) x Skunk #1 (father)

 30-50 g/plant at 3 ft.

 SOG

The Secret ... of Cannabis ... and Highs

...nthal

...s like the *Big Book of Buds* series are possible because of the diversity in marijuana varieties. Think of how different cannabis would be if this were not the case! The terrific subtleties of this plant allow gardeners with different goals to strive for their ideal plant, and marijuana enthusiasts to explore the different effects and odors that this plant has to offer.

We have often heard that varieties of marijuana taste different and create different highs because they contain different ratios of cannabinoids, the chemicals specific to marijuana. However, when modern marijuana was tested for cannabinoids, there was a big spike at delta-9 THC, but all the other cannabinoids, including cannabinol (CBN), cannabdiol (CBD), cannabichromene (CBC) and cannabigerol (CBG) were scarcely noted. In 2005, scientists testing CBD, which was considered the main modifier of THC's effects, noticed that it didn't dock at the CB-1 receptor site in the brain— where THC locks in and sets off the chemical cascade that results in altered awareness. They did find, however, that CBD has many medicinal qualities even though it is not psychoactive.

If cannabinoids other than THC are not causing the high then we must look at other ingredients in the smoke-stream. Terpenes are major components of marijuana resin. These molecules make up the largest percentage of the content of essential oils contained in many plants. Most of them have a boiling point above water, but still readily evaporate in the air. The scents of most flowers, herbs and spices are composed of these oils.

Chemically speaking, terpenes are composed of repeating units of isoprene, which is a five-carbon unit chain or ring with eight hydrogen atoms attached(C_5H_8). Terpenes use the simple isoprene unit as blocks to build 10, 15, 20 and 30 carbon units* and can twist and turn the molecular structure to form simple chains or three-dimensional

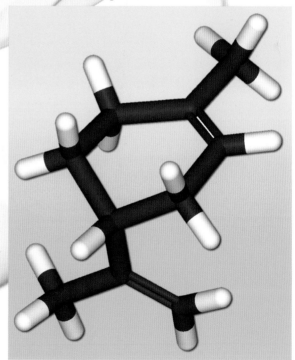

D-Limonene, the terpene with the classic citrus odor. The carbon atoms are black, the attached hydrogen molecules are white (C_{10}, H_{16}).

* These are called, respectively, the C10-monoterpenoid, C15-sesquiterpenoid, C20-diterpenoid, C-30 triterpenoid.

Since plants are not mobile, they can't outrun predators or pick up and relocate when competing plants move into the neighborhood. As a result, they have amassed other defenses against predators and competitors. One of their main strategies is chemical warfare. We use essential oils which are concentrates of compounds designed by plants for various tasks. Some repel enemies, others kill, sicken, delay maturation or affect the metabolism of predators. Plants use other aromatics to attract pollinators for reproduction or to attract enemies' predators.

(polycyclic) structures. In addition, terpenes can form bonds with other molecules, which affect how animals and plants react to them. Depending on how they stack against each other, they form different aromatic compounds.

Most of the aromas that we associate with plants are the result of terpenes and flavonoids. Humans can smell and taste these compounds, but that is not the only ways that they affect us. Aromatherapy uses inhaled essential oils to regulate mood, sleep patterns, acuity, and healing processes. Lavender oil is a soothing agent and relaxant; rosemary is used to focus attention and provide a sense of satisfaction. These effects are a result of the combination of terpenes and other chemicals found in the oils of these plants. While terpenes affect the brain in their own way, they also modify the effect of THC within the brain, adding

subtleties to the high.

Some terpenes may affect the high in this way because they lock into receptor sites in the brain and modify its chemical output. A few, such as thujone, one of the main terpenes in wormwood (which is used to make absinthe), bind weakly to the CB-1 receptor. Others may alter the permeability of cell membranes or the blood brain-barrier, and allow in either more or less THC. Others affect serotonin and dopamine chemistry, by shutting off their production, affecting their movement, binding to their receptor sites, or slowing their natural destruction. Dopamine and serotonin, two of the main regulators of mood and attitude, are affected by some terpenes.

By temporarily altering brain function, terpenes can affect mood, sensitivity, and perception of the senses as well as bodily perceptions such as balance and pain. When terpenes are mixed, as they are in natural plant oils, they each play a role in affecting brain function. Some combinations may work synergistically and others antagonistically, but each "recipe" of terpenes affects moods and feelings in its own way.

Over 100 terpenes have been identified in marijuana. There are actually many more when one considers the multiple variations of each terpene. For instance, the characteristic citrus odor found in fruit rinds differs by type and even variety of fruit— oranges and lemons have different odors, and their terpenes—called limonenes—are mirror versions of each other. Even different varieties of oranges differ in their distinct odor. This is due to slight differences in the amounts of or form of limonene, as well as other compounds that have citrus elements.

About 10-29 percent of marijuana smoke resin is composed of terpenes. Some terpenes present in marijuana appear only occasionally in samples while others are found all the time. The percentage of terpenes and the ratios in which they are found vary by plant variety. You can experience this yourself as different varieties have different smells, indicating a different essential oil makeup.

Age, maturation and time of day of collection can affect the amount and perhaps ratios of terpenes. As plants mature, their odor gets more intense and often changes as they ripen. Climate and weather also affect terpene and flavonoid production. The same variety produces different quantities and perhaps different oils when grown in different soils or with different fertilizers.

Terpenes are constantly being produced but they evaporate under pressure from sunlight and rising temperatures. Plants have more terpenes at the end of the dark period than after a full day of light. You can test this yourself. Check a plant's odor early in the morning and at the end of a sunny day. You will find more pungency early in the morning.

Hops and both groups of Cannabis, low THC hemp and marijuana, contain similar complements of terpenes. One researcher found that the oil of common black pepper (piper nigrum) has a similar group of terpenes as Cannabis. Terpenes are produced in the trichomes, the same glands where THC is produced. They comprise between 10 and 20 percent of the total oils produced by the glands.

The most abundant terpenes in marijuana are described below in general order of abundance. Individual samples may differ widely, both in total percentages of terpenes and in their ratios.

Myrcene is the most prevalent terpene found in most varieties of marijuana but not found in hemp. It is also present in high amounts in hops, lemon grass, West Indian bay tree (used to make bay rum), verbena and the plant from which it derives its name, *mercia*. Myrcene appears in small amounts in the essential oils of many other plants.

Its odor is variously described as clove-like, earthy, green-vegetative, citrus, fruity with tropical mango* and minty nuances. The various odors are the result of

* In fact, Myrcene is found in large quantities in Cavalo, Rosa, Espada and Paulista mangos.

slight differences in the overall essential oil make-up. All of these flavors and odors are commonly used to describe cannabis.

Myrcene is a potent analgesic, anti-inflammatory and antibiotic. It blocks the actions of cytochrome, aflatoxin B and other pro-mutagens that are implicated in carcinogenesis. It is present in small amounts in many essential oils associated with anti-depressive and uplifting behavior.

Myrcene is probably a synergist of THC: A combination of the two molecules creates a stronger experience than THC alone. Myrcene probably affects the permeability of the cell membrane, thus it may allow more THC to reach brain cells.

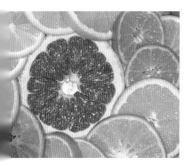

Limonene is found in the rind of citrus and many other fruits and flowers. It is the second, third or fourth most prevalent terpene in cannabis resins. Everyone is familiar with the odor of citrus resins. They explode into the air when a fruit is peeled. The exact odor is determined by the structure of the terpene.

Limonene has anti-bacterial, anti-fungal and anti-cancer activities. It inhibits the Ras cancer gene cascade, which promotes tumor growth. It is used to synergistically promote the absorption of other terpenes by penetrating cell membranes. Limonene sprays are used to treat depression.

Since limonene is such a potent anti-fungal and anti-cancer agent, it is thought to protect against the Aspergillus fungi and carcinogens found in cannabis smoke streams.

Plants use limonene to repulse predators. For instance, flies have a group of receptors similar in function to the taste buds on our tongues. One of them detects noxious chemicals, and responds to limonene as if it were toxic. It is wired directly to the fly brain.

In humans, limonene's design facilitates a direct response by quickly permeating the blood-brain barrier. The result is increased systolic blood pressure. In one test, participants reported subjective alertness and restlessness. Various limonene analogs can cue the brain to sexuality, buoyancy or focused attention.

Caryophyllene is a major terpene found in black pepper (15-25%), clove (10-20%) and cotton (15-25%). It is found in smaller percentages in many other herbs and spices. It has a sweet, woody and dry clove odor and tastes pepper spicy with camphor and astringent citrus backgrounds. It contributes to black pepper's spiciness. The oil is used industrially to enhance tobacco flavor.

Caryophyllene, given in high amounts, is a calcium and potassium ion channel blocker. As a result, it impedes the pressure exerted by heart muscles. As a topical it is analgesic and is one of the active constituents that makes clove oil, a preferred treatment for toothache.

It does not seem to be involved in mood change.

Pinene is the familiar odor associated with pine trees and their resins. It is the major component in turpentine and is found in many other plant essential oils in noticeable amounts including rosemary, sage and eucalyptus. Many additional plant oils contain minute quantities of pinene.

Pinene is used medically as an expectorant and topical antiseptic. It easily crosses the blood-brain barrier where it acts as an acetylcholinesterase inhibitor; that is, it inhibits activity of a chemical that destroys an information transfer molecule. This results in better memory. Largely due to the presence of pinene, rosemary and sage are both considered "memory plants." Concoctions made from their leaves have been used for thousands of years in traditional medicine to retain and restore memory.

Pinene probably gives true skunk varieties, the ones that stink like the animal, much of their odor. It is also a bronchodilator. The smoke seems to expand in your lungs and the high comes on very quickly since a high percentage of the substance will pass into the bloodstream and brain. It also increases focus, self-satisfaction and energy, which seems counterintuitive, but for the presence of terpineol.

Terpineol has a lilac, citrus or apple blossom/lime odor. It is a minor constituent of many plant essential oils. It is used in perfumes and soaps for fragrance.

Terpineol is obtained commercially from processing other terpenes. It reduces motility—the capability for movement—by 45% in rat tests.

This may account for the couch-lock effects of some cannabis although that odor is not usually associated with body highs. However, terpineol is often found in cannabis with high pinene levels. Its odor would be masked by the pungent woodsy aromas of pinene.

Borneol smells much like the menthol aroma of camphor and is easily converted into it. It is found in small quantities in many essential oils. Commercially, it is derived from *artemisia* plants such as wormwood and some species of cinnamon.

It is considered a "calming sedative" in Chinese medicine. It is directed for fatigue, recovery from illness and stress.

The camphor-like overtones of Silver Haze varieties are unmistakable. The high does have a calming effect as well as its psychedelic aspects. This probably means that there is a large amount of borneol present.

Delta 3-Carene has a sweet pungent odor. It is a constituent of pine and cedar resin but is found in many other plants including rosemary. In aromatherapy, cypress oil, high in D-3-Carene, is used to dry excess fluids, tears, running noses, excess menstrual flow and perspiration. It may contribute to the dry eye and dry mouth experienced by marijuana users.

Linalool has a floral scent reminiscent of spring flowers such as lily of the valley, but with spicy overtones. It is refined from lavender, neroli and other essential oils. Humans can detect its odor at rates as low as one part per million in the air.

Linalool is being tested now for treatment of several types of cancers. It is also a component of several sedating essential oils. In tests on humans who inhaled it, it caused severe sedation. In tests on rats, it reduced their activity by almost 75 percent.

Pulegone has a minty-camphor odor and flavor that is used in the candy industry. It is implicated in liver damage when used in very high dosages. It is found in tiny quantities in marijuana.

Pulegone is an acetylcholinesterase inhibitor. That is, it stops the action of the protein that destroys acetylcholine, which is used by the brain to store memories. It may counteract THC's activity, which leads to low acetylcholine levels. The result is that you'd forget more on THC alone than THC accompanied by pulegone.

1,8-Cineole is the main ingredient in oil of eucalyptus. It has a camphor-minty odor. It is also found in other fragrant plants and in minor amounts in marijuana. It is used to increase circulation, pain relief and has other topical uses.

Cineole easily crosses the blood-brain-barrier and triggers a fast olfactory reaction. Eucalyptus oil is considered centering, balancing and stimulating. It is probably the stimulating and thought provoking part of the cannabis smoke stream.

Terpenes and their interactions with each other and resultant effect on brain activities is a fascinating territory, and another level of exploration and creativity for seed breeders. By learning the odors of the terpenes, you may be able to predict the mind-altering properties each lends to a bud.

Mapping the Pot Palate

DJ Short

The breeding and production of fine cannabis is more art than science. A creative mind and sense of intuition are necessary to achieve success in this field. While some herb is strictly pleasing to the mental palate, taste can also be tantamount to the buzz for the cannabis connoisseur.

The range of flavors expressed by the genus cannabis is extraordinary. No other plant on the planet can equal the cacophony of smells and tastes available from cannabis. The spectrum of possible smells and tastes a human can experience is large and complex. To date, no one has created a fully usable olfaction chart, although Ann Noble of the wine world has developed a nifty "aroma wheel" for that industry, which inspired me to develop a similar map for cannabis. Like its counterpart, categories branch out from the general to the more specific. For instance, a category like "fruity" will subdivide into "berry" and "citrus;" citrus divides further into the more distinct flavors of "lemon," "lime" and "orange."

The range of aromas and flavors represented on the chart (next page) are all possible to achieve. Some of these are already well known and represented among widely available cannabis varieties, while others require some cross-breeding to achieve. Some of the most desirable bud bridges multiple categories, creating a complex sensory experience. Although the strength of smell and flavor may vary, many strains' flavors were best expressed when they were grown outdoors in their region of origin. Note that aroma and flavor vary by growing method and also between various stages of the plant. The aroma of a live bud on the plant, a dried and cured bud, and the smoke on the inhale and exhale, may all be different from each other.

The physical palate of cannabis is a wondrous dimension, important in distinguishing the good from the superb in the weed world. Capable of being refined, one's palate is best educated through experience. The map that follows is meant to aid the discriminating stoner in charting the territory. Happy travels.

Mapping the Pot Palate: What's your favorite flavor?

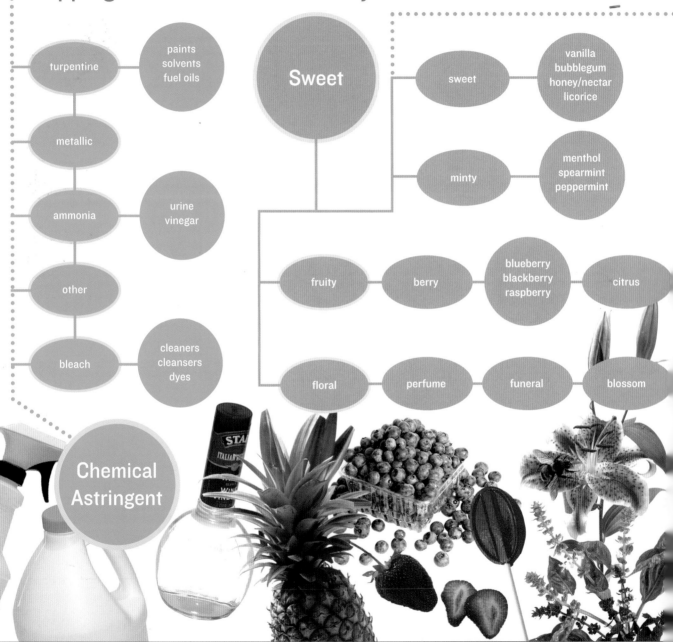

turpentine — paints, solvents, fuel oils

metallic

ammonia — urine, vinegar

other

bleach — cleaners, cleansers, dyes

Sweet

sweet — vanilla, bubblegum, honey/nectar, licorice

minty — menthol, spearmint, peppermint

fruity — berry — blueberry, blackberry, raspberry — citrus

floral — perfume — funeral — blossom

Chemical Astringent

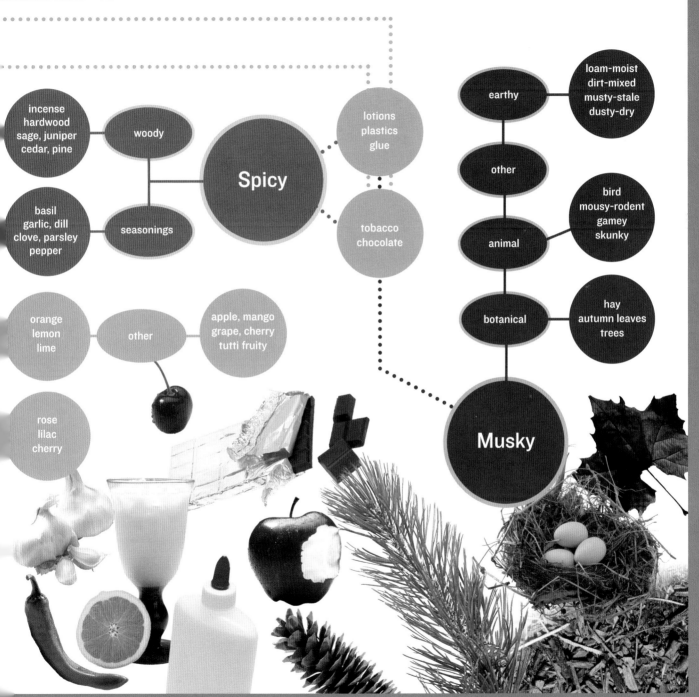

incense
hardwood
sage, juniper
cedar, pine

woody

basil
garlic, dill
clove, parsley
pepper

seasonings

Spicy

lotions
plastics
glue

tobacco
chocolate

earthy

loam-moist
dirt-mixed
musty-stale
dusty-dry

other

animal

bird
mousy-rodent
gamey
skunky

orange
lemon
lime

other

apple, mango
grape, cherry
tutti fruity

botanical

hay
autumn leaves
trees

rose
lilac
cherry

Musky

Fruity Thai
Ceres Seeds

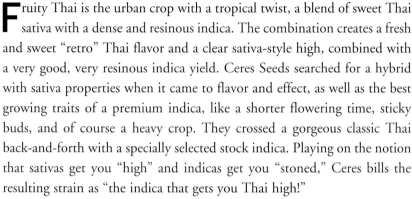

Fruity Thai is the urban crop with a tropical twist, a blend of sweet Thai sativa with a dense and resinous indica. The combination creates a fresh and sweet "retro" Thai flavor and a clear sativa-style high, combined with a very good, very resinous indica yield. Ceres Seeds searched for a hybrid with sativa properties when it came to flavor and effect, as well as the best growing traits of a premium indica, like a shorter flowering time, sticky buds, and of course a heavy crop. They crossed a gorgeous classic Thai back-and-forth with a specially selected stock indica. Playing on the notion that sativas get you "high" and indicas get you "stoned," Ceres bills the resulting strain as "the indica that gets you Thai high!"

Indoors, Fruity Thai delivers both quality and quantity. This variety also produces amazing results in the greenhouse. While flowering, Fruity Thai looks much like a sativa plant, with a single large main cola and long, thinner branches around the base. Like a pure sativa, she still stretches a little at the start. As she matures, her buds build up from tight clusters of flowers into compact pointy cones that weigh in at comfortable yields of one gram per watt of light. Fruity Thai plants take only 8-9 weeks to mature.

Fruity Thai buds are covered with thousands of tiny, but clear, THC crystals, making them look like a starry night against a dark green sky. Besides her glittering and weighty harvest, the most notable features of this variety are her scent and flavor. Fruity Thai produces little odor while flowering, but once the buds are ripe, they release a noticeable fresh and fruity scent. The taste has overtones of lemon and melon. The effect of Fruity Thai is a comfortable, dreamy, but functional high. The vibe is sensual and communicative, happy and playful.

Fruity Thai took home Second Place in the indica category at the 2006 High Times Cannabis Cup, and proved a popular party favor at the Grass-A-Matazz Jazz 'n' Grass party afterwards, sponsored in part by Ceres Seeds.

 50/50

 active, sensual, talkative

 lemon, melon

 50-65 days/Oct.

 Thai sativa x Dutch indica

 1 g/w of lights 400 g/plant out

 in/out greenhouse

 SOG

Ceres Seeds

Ceres Seeds is a 100% homegrown Dutch seed company. Its history goes back to 1988 when its owners started their first seeds and cuttings. One of the founders became a bit of an urban legend when he went to buy cuttings and growing supplies at Positronics—with his grandmother! The Ceres Seeds guys were learning the ropes back then. In the early 1990s, they worked for the old, infamous Dreadlock Coffeeshop, as well as reputable seed companies like the Sensi Seed Bank, where they learned how to produce and cross good, healthy plants, and how to know good cannabis when they saw it.

Ceres' original seeds came from the imported Jamaican, Thai, and Colombian weed that formed the stock of many coffeeshops in Amsterdam before the modern varieties took over. With a little help from their friends throughout the Dutch cannabis industry, Ceres Seeds also acquired some indica-dominant varieties that had been in already Holland for many generations.

In the late 1990s, seed companies started popping up everywhere. The guys at Ceres Seeds were surprised that many of these companies were making F2 varieties (hybrids crossed with hybrids). They decided get serious and jump in the game, making their own varieties. They approached breeding with the simple philosophy of simple, reliable and 100% stable strains. They started with landrace genetics that were available from Sensi, plus the good indica seeds they had collected over the years in Holland. "Then," says Ceres, "we remembered the old sativa seeds from all those baggies of weed we had smoked ten or fifteen years earlier. We started testing, growing, experimenting, selecting and reproducing using the best seeds from all our collections." In 1999 they made the big step and started Ceres Seeds. They took the name from Ceres, the Roman goddess of agriculture and motherly love. Her name derives from the Proto-Indo-European root "ker," meaning "to grow," which is also the root for the words "create" and "increase."

Ceres' first F1 variety, White Smurf, was introduced in 2000. With the invaluable help of the well-known "Smurf" name from an established local coffeeshop, this variety won two awards at the High Times Cannabis Cup that year. This gave Ceres the encouragement they needed. They continued to work on their prize stock and added other varieties such as Northern Lights x Skunk #1, Ceres Kush, and White Indica to their offerings.

Hempshopper, a great hemp and cannabis gift shop that opened its doors on the Nieuwezijds Voorburgwal in 2004, is home to Ceres Seeds in Amsterdam. From here, Ceres Seeds helped produce the first Grass-A-Matazz in 2005. The Grass-A-Matazz is a Jazz 'n' Grass party, featuring the legendary John Sinclair. It is held during the annual High Times Cannabis Cup, and represents the blues and jazz roots in our cannabis history. At the first party, Ceres presented their new variety Fruity Thai (see preceding page). The following year, this strain won Second Prize at the Cannabis Cup in the indica category.

G-Bomb

Big Buddha Seeds

From the underground networks of the UK arose a cutting that became the infamous "G," also known as G-Force. G's origins are unknown, but it has been making the rounds since the early 1990s. Rumors or educated guesses as to its composition have included Sensi's G-13 indica and Flying Dutchmen's spicy Pot of Gold, but these are unverified. Such guesses are based on the qualities that G shares in common with superstar Dutch indicas—a hardy and vigorous dark indica growth pattern, a unique effervescent quality, and a decidedly spicy hash taste.

When G-Force made it into the hands of Big Buddha, it was considered worthwhile to develop. Big Buddha feminized G by crossing it with a reversed G clone father, resulting in all-female, all-G strain, the G-Bomb. As a hefty indica, G-Bomb is a high yielding plant that forms gigantic colas the size of one's forearm. This plant likes to form a dense and impressive main central bud, making it a very solid choice for sea of green setups. If sea of green is unappealing, not to worry. Over many years, this strain has been grown in just about every common method from screen of green, big pots, hydro, coco, you name it—and its solid indica diligence leads it to perform admirably across the board. As such, it is a good plant to build up a beginner's confidence.

G-Bomb loves to be fed well and eats heavily. Indoor plants finish in 8–10 weeks, and outdoor plants can be harvested at the end of October. A little temperature variability is all right as long as the weather stays above freezing. G-Bomb maintains a steady monochromatic green, even when the nights turn cool. These plants also stay pretty short; at maximum outdoor sizes, they are still under the 6-foot mark (around 1.8 meters) at finish. Certainly size matters, but the right kind of size—not plant size, but bud size! This is where G-Bomb cashes in, delivering outdoor yields of up to 900 grams (nearly 2 pounds) per plant.

The G-Bomb aroma has been best described as dank lemony hashish. The citrus bite and an edge of spice will come through in the flavor. G-Bomb is a deep stone, with sedative potency. It is a great addition to the medicine stash of chronic pain sufferers, insomniacs, or others who want the soothing effects of a heavy, slow-release body indica.

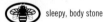 sleepy, body stone

 lemon hash

 56–70 days

 ♀ G x ♂ reversed G clone

 400g per plant in 1000g per plant out

Grape Krush
DJ Short

Photo: Ed Rosenthal

Grape Krush belongs to the Blueberry family bred by DJ Short. The Blueberry strains mix indica with haze for a combination of happy stone and easy, adaptable cultivation. Specifically, the indica genes give the plants a shorter growing season than the slow-growing and sometimes finicky hazes. Blueberries tend toward a blue tint in the leaves and a berry flavor in the smoke. Within the Blueberry family, Grape Krush is the peaceful child. This strain's high is physically soothing, but still haze-y enough to keep a conversation flowing.

Grape Krush was developed for indoor growing, but can flourish outdoors as well—even as far north as Holland—especially if given organic nutrients. Indoors, she prefers soil but adapts well to hydroponic systems, too. In general, DJ Short recommends light feeding with nitrogen and organic nutrients; however, Grape Krush loves all of the good worm castings and bat guano she can get.

 60/40

 sedate, social, creeper

 musky, sweet

 55-65 days/
mid-Sept.-mid-Oct.

 Blueberry line parents

 25-50 g/ft.²

Grape Krush branches bushy, especially when topped. Like her Blueberry relatives, she is dark green to purple with lavender/red hues. She has thicker and more variegated leaves than the other Blueberries. The larger calyxes on her bulkier, more "rounded" buds show a distinctive fox-tailing structure late in her flowering cycle. Her variegated leaves sometimes curl or "krinkle;" this is an expression of anomalous recessed traits from her diverse ancestors, not a mutation that indicates an unhealthy plant.

Grape Krush finishes in approximately 8-9 weeks indoors, or from late September to mid-late October outdoors. She is medium in height and heavy in yield—25 to 50 grams (1-2 oz.) per square foot at 50 watts per square foot, or up to 1 gram per watt under optimal conditions.

Growing plants have a strong odor, both sweet and musky. The harvest from this strain is connoisseur-grade bud with a sweetish smoke. The high comes on very slowly, building up for as much as an hour, and then settles in for the night – a bit more like a pot brownie stone than the usual smoker's rush. Traces of haze in the stone add inspiration to the conversation, and some radiant dreams or fantasies at bedtime. It's a relaxing and social effect, like red wine, and a good antidote to social anxiety.

Hash Plant
Sensi Seed Bank

Hash Plant derives from the famed indoor Hash Plant cutting that traveled to Holland from the Northwest U.S in the 1980s. This hybrid was crossed to one of the three genotypes of the super Afghanis, Northern Lights #1, to produce an impressively strong indica specimen.

Named for its hashy-tasting, highly resinous buds, the Hash Plant has been known as an important building block for other Sensi Seeds hybrids for many years, but has rarely been made available outside of the Cannabis Castle breeding program. It was reintroduced to the market by the Sensi Seed Bank in 1999.

Expect a short indica-type plant that averages 3-4 feet (100-130 cm) in height, with a gratifyingly quick finish, a pleasantly narcotic high, and of course, great hashmaking potential.

While an indoor breed in the Dutch climate, this plant has fared well in dry latitudes such as the Mediterranean. All indoor growing methods are suitable, although Sensi growers like the hydro culture garden method best. Hash Plant is easy to clone, offering you a simple method for multiplying your success.

(I)

 body stone

 sweet/spicy

 40-45 days

 Original Hash Plant x Hash Plant/ Northern Lights #1 hybrid

 380 g per m²

 SOG

Photo: Nadim Sabella

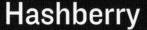

Hashberry

Mandala Seeds

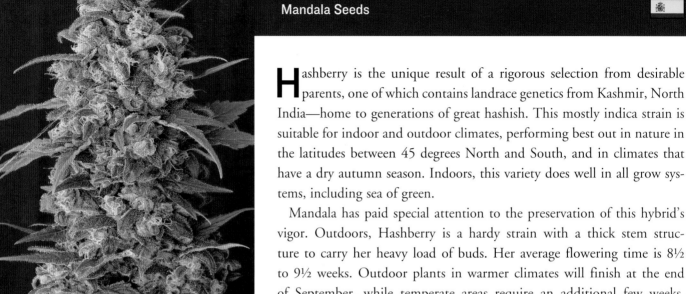

mostly indica

relaxing, head/body balance

blackcurrent jam, hashy

60-65 days

♀ indica from California x ♂ strain with land race genetics from Kashmir, North India

450-500 g/m²

below 45°N latitude

Hashberry is the unique result of a rigorous selection from desirable parents, one of which contains landrace genetics from Kashmir, North India—home to generations of great hashish. This mostly indica strain is suitable for indoor and outdoor climates, performing best out in nature in the latitudes between 45 degrees North and South, and in climates that have a dry autumn season. Indoors, this variety does well in all grow systems, including sea of green.

Mandala has paid special attention to the preservation of this hybrid's vigor. Outdoors, Hashberry is a hardy strain with a thick stem structure to carry her heavy load of buds. Her average flowering time is 8½ to 9½ weeks. Outdoor plants in warmer climates will finish at the end of September, while temperate areas require an additional few weeks. Flowering times outdoors can be shortened by as much as two weeks if well established clones are transplanted around summer solstice. In organic indoor grows, you can almost do without feeding; an adequate pot size and quality potting soil is all you need for optimal results.

Mandala recommends allowing seedlings to reach 8-10 inches (20-25 cm) and then forcing flowering. Using this method, growers can expect an average yield of 450-500 grams (16-18 oz.) per square meter under 400 watts per square meter. This is an easy plant to grow and shows good heat resistance. Its medium-sized stature makes Hashberry a good selection when space is at a premium. There are two distinct phenotypes: one is shorter and develops branches that reach up to the middle of the plant; the other is slightly taller with almost no branching. Both are perfect for close planting, but the branchy type should be given a bit of extra space for better light dispersal.

Hashberry carries an extremely heavy main cola that dominates the plant structure and contributes to her above-average yields. The cola offers a delicious aroma, and old school high and taste. Many old-timers have reported that smoking this strain reminds them of the finest Columbian grass of the 1970s, an effect Mandala refers to as "vintage deja-vú." This strain is easy to trim and the dried buds have great "bag appeal."

Young flowering plants develop a fruity-floral aroma that smells like blueberry or blackcurrent jam. Some plants have a more spicy note mixed in with the fruity-floral bouquet. As flowering and resin production progresses, a hashy aroma also sets in. Other plants have a minty-peppery taste to them that is equally pleasant.

As the name suggests, Hashberry is a great variety for the hashish fan. The high starts out very clear and builds slowly into a classic chill-out vibe with a relaxing and balanced head-body effect. Toward the end, a more body-oriented phase sets in that nevertheless leaves you able to be social and active. Hashberry is perfect when used to relax and unwind in the evening, or to alleviate stress and pain.

Hawaiian Snow
Greenhouse Seed Co.

In the commercial seed world, this strain is as rare as snow in Hawaii—a long season equatorial with a triple-haze parentage. Hazes are popular for their light fresh taste and radiant highs, but they require more care and patience than the usual fare of commercially available strains.

Hawaiian Snow's lengthy ripening time confines her indoors except in the most favorable climates. Large and rangy, she should be grown under 18 hours of light for a short vegetative period. Hawaiian Snow's size and slow flowering make her unsuitable for sea of green setups. This variety needs a big pot of soil with a low acid content (starting at a pH of 6.0). Flowering takes at least 14 weeks. Growers can smoke their faster strains while anticipating Snow's payoff – the mental dawn that only comes from slow-ripening hazes.

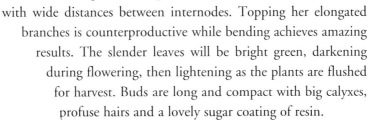

Hawaiian Snow grows in a pine-tree profile, with wide distances between internodes. Topping her elongated branches is counterproductive while bending achieves amazing results. The slender leaves will be bright green, darkening during flowering, then lightening as the plants are flushed for harvest. Buds are long and compact with big calyxes, profuse hairs and a lovely sugar coating of resin.

Hawaiian Snow's rich spicy sativa taste leaves some mint freshness behind on exhale. Its complex mix of aromas and flavors evokes eucalyptus, lemon grass and a hint of musk and green moss. As the flavor fades, the high reveals itself: the body stays alert while the moods and thoughts enter a space of elation, which encourages freethinking and a sense of wellbeing. It is a lovely social high that lowers tensions and incites laughter.

Hawaiian Snow won 1st prize (overall) at the 2003 *High Times* Cannabis Cup.

 90/10

 creative, cerebral, creeper

 herbal fresh and minty

 105-112 days indoors

 ♀ Hawaiian Haze x ♀ Pure Haze x ♂ Neville's Haze

 100 to 120 grams (3-4 oz.) per plant (5 gal. pots)

Photo: Nadim Sabella

Headband
DNA Genetics/Reserva Privada

Imagine, if you will, throwing caution and all fashion sense to the wind, and donning a headband à la John McEnroe in the early '80s or Luke Wilson in the Royal Tennenbaums—or for the ladies, Olivia Newton-John aerobics-video style. The Headband is like a reassuring little brain hug, and its presence may bring a heightened awareness of the gray matter. Imagine a strain that, when smoked, mimics that feeling, moving rapidly from the front of the mind to the back, easing anxiety while inducing awareness. Now you have the idea.

The Headband is a brilliant case of reverse engineering by DNA Genetics. A choice, unidentified strain nicknamed the 707 Headband was making the circuit and gaining attention for its combination of potency and dank flavor. DNA breeders made some educated guesses about the parents of the 707 Headband, and then worked on recreating a strain from scratch that mimicked the 707's superb qualities.

 70/30

 mellow, relaxing

 fuel-sour

 63–70 days

 ♀ Sour Diesel x ♂ OG Kush

 500–600g per m²

This Headband's Sour Diesel/OG Kush combination brings together many admirable qualities from its already notorious parent strains. This is an agreeable squatty, bushy plant that makes the most of the available space. In the vegetative phase, it grows fast and spreads wide when allowed to go au naturale, producing many tops and an even canopy with minimal coaxing. At maturity, the size roughly doubles. This plant does not grow as tall as Sour Diesel or as stretchy as the OG Kush, and is less picky about the nutrients. Straight out of the gate, Headband is very pungent and colorful, taking a pinkish turn around the 4th week and gaining a wow factor with photo-worthy tones of blue, purple, and deep dark red in the last two weeks of ripening.

When finished, the Headband has great bag and head appeal. Its uniquely enjoyable fuel-sour taste makes it memorable. Soil does the best job in bringing out the flavor, but this plant produces good yields of high-grade medicine in coco, hydro, or other soilless methods so long as the plants are flushed with pH-balanced water for two weeks prior to harvest. The high is not too overpowering, and lasts a long time, making it a good utility daytime smoke. Headband is good for reducing anxiety. The beginner or hobby medical grower will find that this plant cooperates in the garden and delivers high quality yields.

3rd place, 2009 Cannabis Cup, coffeeshop category.

UPDATE: DNA currently provides Headband genetics under the name Sour Kush.

Headband Story
DNA Genetics

The Headband name was actually inspired by an orphan strain of unknown parentage making the rounds about town and eventually making it to marijuana communities around the globe. This mystery strain, called the 707 Headband, was creating a stir with its combination of high-end features. It was a clone-only strain whose origins were unknown, and no one seemed to know the parentage. It was clear why people liked the 707 Headband: the fuel-like flavor was great, reminiscent of the Diesels with some Kush overtones. When the connoisseur breeders at DNA Genetics got a taste, they decided to put their powers of discrimination to work. In their estimation, 707 Headband tasted like a cross of OG Kush and Sour Diesel.

The OG Kush and Sour Diesel had both originated as great finds from bag seed, but the Headband had no seed to work with. DNA did not have any 707 genetics as seeds or clones to work from. Instead they put their expertise to work in breeding, using what they thought would best mimic the 707 Headband's genetics. The DNA Genetics Headband is only a form of flattery to its namesake, the original 707. The DNA Headband was created by reversing the OG Kush to pollinate the Sour Diesel. Next DNA breeders selected from the cross in order to produce the closest match to the 707 they could muster. People who smoke DNA Headband overwhelmingly agree that its flavor, look, smell, and density are a near-exact twin of the original 707. The pinkish color of the nuggs will also dazzle and amaze. Headband won 3rd place at the 2009 Cannabis Cup.

Ice
Nirvana Seed Bank

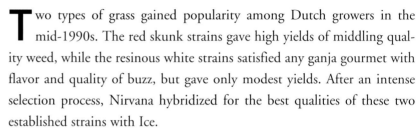

Two types of grass gained popularity among Dutch growers in the mid-1990s. The red skunk strains gave high yields of middling quality weed, while the resinous white strains satisfied any ganja gourmet with flavor and quality of buzz, but gave only modest yields. After an intense selection process, Nirvana hybridized for the best qualities of these two established strains with Ice.

A new generation power plant, Ice weds kind bud with kind yields. Ice has few branches, minimal foliage, and many floral clusters: a plus when manicuring. Virtually all of the branches Ice extends will be heavily budded. A rapid grower, this plant can be put directly into flower after roots are established. She will double in height and start forming flowers in the first 2 weeks of the 12 hour light regimen. No ice maiden, this strain is happiest with lots of fresh, warm humid air circulating around her. Hydroponic methods will give the most effective results with the best resin production. A sea of green set-up is appropriate.

Ice practically fumes with the nearly fuel-like scent of raw THC. Flavored like Nepali black hash, toking Ice is likely to induce coughing. Plan on putting your brain on ice because this variety's heavy stone may leave you in a lazy daze for hours.

Winner, *High Times* Cannabis Cup 1998

 stoney, body high

 fuel, hashy

 63-70 days

 Skunk sort & White family strain

 600g per m²

 SOG

Iranian Autoflower
Dr. Greenthumb Seeds

Iran is also widely known as Persia. This home to one of the world's oldest known continuous major civilizations has a long history with cannabis, and in particular with hashish, including tales that date back a thousand years. The country of Iran is roughly the size of the UK, or slightly bigger than the state of Alaska. It is southeast of Kazakhstan and Russia, two countries believed to be the birthplace of autoflowering strains. Iran has coastline along the Caspian Sea in the north and the Persian Gulf in the south, but is probably more known for being sandwiched between Iraq and Afghanistan. Much like these neighbors, Iran has much mountainous terrain, which turns to desert as one moves south and east.

Dr. Greenthumb's Iranian Autoflower strain is an all-indica strain with parents from the rugged terrain of Iran. It was developed for outdoor use in temperate climates. This lush green plant will grow anywhere, and finishes in just 90 days from start to finish. The Iranian Autoflower is compact, growing between 3–4 feet in most gardens, although it can reach heights of 5 feet at maximum. This variety tends to keep branching minimal and focus most of its energy on developing a single dominant cola.

This plant can finish in 3 months from seed to harvest, spending about half of that time in flowering. Since this is an autoflowering strain, the plants shift into flower development without strict light cycles, making it an easy plant to grow outdoors. Multiple harvests are possible from spring thaw to the first freeze of late autumn, and the lack of light requirements allows harvesting to occur in months during which outdoor harvests are uncommon, reducing many of the threats created by a more predictable schedule.

In addition, these plants are highly resistant to cold weather and only have minimal smell while growing. When combined with potential off season harvesting and compact size, they offer an impressive stealthiness for outdoor growers.

Iranian Autoflower buds form tight dense nuggets that take on golden hues as they cure. Average per-plant yields are 4–8 ounces. Iranian Autoflower reflects the long hashish tradition of its native region. In a side-by-side comparison, testers equated this all-indica strain's potency to White Widow and OG Kush. The deep earthy tones bring out flavors reminiscent of hashish, and the smoke has strong narcotic and pain-relieving qualities that lead card carrying med-users to ask for it by name.

 pain relief, sedating

 hashy, earthy

 40–50 days

 ♀Iranian x ♂NA S1

 100–200g per plant

Jack F6
Sannie's Seeds

Jack Herer has become a classic strain known for its freshness and uplifting effects. The original Jack Herer variety combined a multiple-hybrid Haze with a sativa-indica Skunk. Sannie's Jack was developed to create a consistently sativa-dominant Jack Herer variety. Both parents come from inbred lines of Sannie's Jack.

Sannie's Jack F6 develops like a real sativa, with thin leaves and fast growth. It is advisable to not vegetate these ladies for too long since they continue to grow for 4 weeks after the 12/12 lighting switch. While they do shoot up quickly, Sannie's Jack F6 is not a branchy plant and tends to form a big main bud, making it suitable to a sea of green method. Nine plants per square meter are recommended for maximizing space without overcrowding. Screen of green growing techniques also work well.

Sannie's Jack F6 forms big foxtail buds that build up a heavy coat of trichomes. The buds are compact and powerful, like a bodybuilder's upper arm. These colas require support structures to keep them upright. The foliage stays an intense green during flowering.

Average yields in a well tended garden range around an impressive 600 grams (over a pound) per square meter.

These translucent crystal-dense buds produce a clear, up high that comes on steadily and has a high ceiling, continuing to build over a long period of time. The citrus tones are strong but not aggressive or overly acrid, leading

to a very light, smooth smoke. Those who like a psychedelic leaning, euphoric buzz that lends itself to creative activities will find this variety delivers an especially pleasant experience.

 active, alert, happy, psychedelic

 citrus, fresh, spicy

 84–98 days

 ♀ Sannie's Jack F5 x ♂ Sannie's Jack F4

 500–750g per m²

 SOG

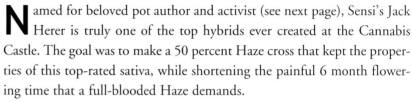

Jack Herer

Sensi Seed Bank

Named for beloved pot author and activist (see next page), Sensi's Jack Herer is truly one of the top hybrids ever created at the Cannabis Castle. The goal was to make a 50 percent Haze cross that kept the properties of this top-rated sativa, while shortening the painful 6 month flowering time that a full-blooded Haze demands.

This variety's long-fingered leaves and dense, grape-cluster bud formations appear light green due to the frosty resin coating. The few hairs on the buds turn brick red as the plant matures. The smell is fresh with a signature Haze accent and a pleasing hint of skunkiness. Since the rooted clones can go directly into flowering, the total number of light hours in the life cycle is almost exactly the same as a conventional indica-heavy cross, even though the flowering cycle is longer.

If growing in soil, full ground is recommended over pots, which are usually too small. Dry climates, like Spain and California are Jack Herer's only reasonable candidates for an outdoor home. Growing Jack indoors is necessary in most parts of the world. Hydroponics will give quick satisfying results, but Jack Herer is best grown as bigger plants.

A longer-flowering cross can be unnerving to grow, but bravery and patience will be rewarded with fresh peppery buds that produce an immediate cerebral, up high. Don't cave to the temptation and harvest too early. When allowed its full time to ripen, Jack Herer is a tasty smoke with mild lung expansion and possibly visually enhancing or silly effects.

Winner, *High Times* Cannabis Cup 1995

 cerebral, up

 fresh, peppery

 65–75 days

 Secret multiple hybrid Haze x Red Skunk strain

 450g per m

Long Live the Hemperor, Jack Herer!

By Bonnie King

"Because of one man's inspiration and stubborn refusal to accept anything less than legal cannabis, the movement has excelled beyond expectations."

Jack at the Seattle Hempfest. Photo: Subcool

When Jack Herer spoke about hemp, everyone listened. A devoted cannabis warrior Jack unwaveringly believed that the cannabis plant, a renewable source of fuel, food and medicine, should be legal to grow and consume. He was outwardly dismayed with the US government, which he said hid the facts from American citizens. His book *The Emperor Wears No Clothes* was originally published in 1985 in order to make this unknown information widely available. It became the seminal book on the history of hemp and marijuana prohibition.

This book is considered a "Bible" of cannabis facts, and continues to be used as an essential research tool and catalyst in the advocacy to decriminalize cannabis. Everyone in the know has heard of it, read it, shared it, or referred to it in the debate over the merits of this plant. In fact, many of the most widely circulated arguments touting the benefits of cannabis entered the cultural consciousness with Jack's book. He soon earned the nickname "the Hemperor."

"Jack was basically on a book tour for 30 years," said Ed Rosenthal. "Many don't recognize that hemp is where it is because of Jack. He worked for this, and now it's happening: hemp is an available product, and prohibition is on its way out."

The Beginning

Jack spent the early 1970s in Venice Beach, California, where he opened two head shops. In 1973, he published his first book, *G.R.A.S.S. (Great Revolutionary American Standard System)*, and met his friend and mentor Edwin M. Adair, aka "Captain Ed." Captain Ed changed Jack's life, bringing enlightenment to what Jack

Jack in his younger days. Photo: courtesy Jeannie Herer and Nicki Duzy.

had already learned about the far-reaching benefits of the hemp plant.

"Once he had this inspiration, the 'aha' moment,

Jack and Ed Rosenthal

Jack Herer shouted his message from the rooftops, becoming the most well-known hemp activist in the world.

A Man and a Mission

A gregarious, bombastic man, Jack left an impression with everyone he met. As an activist he was a force to be reckoned with. Jack would take on a whole room full of naysayers and come out ahead. He insisted that hemp and cannabis groups alike support marijuana in all its forms, and he was happy to debate the issue. He once chided the Hemp Industries Association because he felt they were trying to separate the hemp cause from the more controversial marijuana issue in order to legitimate their cause. Jack felt they could not turn a blind eye to marijuana arrests and imprisonments and succeed. His message to hemp activists and entrepreneurs was this: "Until these people are out of jail, until this plant is legal in all its forms, you guys have a responsibility!"

There were those with whom Jack did not see eye-to-eye, but they found harmony by focusing on common goals. Chris Conrad, editor of the first edition of *The Emperor Wears No Clothes,* said the first time he met Jack, the two of them were arguing within minutes. "If you never got mad at Jack, and Jack never got mad at you, then you probably didn't know Jack very well." Jack was a good friend and a good guy to have on your side. Certainly, he was a lot of fun to smoke marijuana with! He had an indisputable talent for bringing all sides to the table.

Some stoner lore tells of Ed Rosenthal and Jack being super critical of each other. Ed says this is categor-

everything changed," Ed Rosenthal said. "Jack saw the relationship with marijuana and hemp—that they had a similar destiny: if one is outlawed, so is the other; if one is legal, so will be the other. He had a profound understanding of the intricate connection between the medicinal herb and the industrial plant that required they be addressed as together."

In 1974, when Jack was 34, he and Captain Ed made their famous pact. In Jack's own words: "We swore to work every day to legalize marijuana and get all pot prisoners out of jail until we were dead, marijuana was legal, or until we turned 84 when we could quit. We didn't have to quit, but we could." True to their word, they worked together on the issue until Captain Ed's untimely death at age 50 from leukemia in 1994. After Ed's death, Jack continued with their mission and lived on to fulfill their pledge.

ically untrue. "It never got to anything like that. We had intellectual arguments only; we were never rivals. We were two co-revolutionaries working on different aspects of the same project."

Jack Herer's mission was driven not by a desire for fame or fortune, but rather by his unyielding determination to end hemp prohibition and thus right a wrong that had unfolded from a distorted misdirection in America's political history. Like many, Jack understood that US policies on hemp and cannabis were illogical and even detrimental to the earth. "It is the safest, smartest, best medicine on the planet,"

Jack and Subcool share a bowl. Photo: MzJill

Jack said. "You'd have to be stupid not to use it!"

Many know Jack Herer's name not for his activism, but for a high-grade strain of cannabis from Sensi Seeds with sativa dominant characteristics, named in honor of Jack's work. It is a complex strain that requires some gardening talent to grow it optimally, yet people love it because of its mentally stimulating and uplifting high that is fresh with a peppery bite. In these qualities, it shares much with Jack Herer, the man. The Jack Herer strain has won several awards, including the 7th High Times Cannabis Cup, the "Academy Awards of Marijuana." It has also become a popular choice as a parent strain with its mix of old-school skunk and the ever-popular west coast haze. Because of its genetic diversity, many Jack variants have also emerged on the market, bringing out different facets of the cross.

In his book Jack reiterates cannabis' low risk use, "A smoker would theoretically have to consume nearly 1,500 pounds of marijuana within about fifteen minutes to induce a lethal response." Jack offered a reward of $100,000 to anyone who could prove marijuana had killed a user. To this day, no one has tried to collect.

Every year, Jack and his crew would travel thousands of miles making appearances, book signings, and speaking engagements at hemp festivals and other events. Jack met hundreds of people a day, and to all of them he had the same message: hemp will save the world.

He was also a pivotal figure in the fight for medical marijuana. In 1996, Jack assisted Dennis Peron in the passing of California Proposition 215. Ending prohibition was still a few giant steps away, but Jack was adamant that it was within reach—closer, with each educated voter. Jack was very opposed to taxing marijuana and became more fixed in his position with age. However, he understood progress, and the sacrifices required for advancement.

In 2000, the Hemperor suffered a heart attack and a major stroke resulting in long-term rehab for on-

Jack was a good friend and a good guy to have on your side. Certainly, he was a lot of fun to smoke marijuana with! He had an indisputable talent for bringing all sides to the table.

Jack showing me his hemp boxers, 2008 Photo: Austin King

going speaking difficulties and loss of mobility. He was back in action after three years. In May 2004, he revealed that treatment with the *aminita muscaria*, a psychoactive mushroom was the secret to his recovery and the subject of an upcoming book. Jack was back and going strong.

Jack's tireless efforts did not go unnoticed by the larger cannabis community. In 2003, Herer was inducted into the Counterculture Hall of Fame at the 16th Cannabis Cup in recognition of his first book *G.R.A.S.S.* An award was also established in his name in 2004 by Patient Alliance.

By 2009, Jack was back in full swing. He was speaking more clearly and said he felt better than he had in years. On September 12th of that year, he was at HempStalk in Portland, Oregon, where he was anxious to discuss the medicinal success of Rick Simpson's Healing Hemp Oil, whom he expected to join on a European tour weeks later. He was enthusiastic about the future.

On that fateful day, Jack encouraged the audience at HempStalk to continue the fight, to see the current marijuana initiatives through to success, and to resist the temptation to agree to pay the government to use cannabis. "I don't want to give the United States government one fucking dollar of taxes. I think they should go to jail for getting you and me and 20 million other people arrested for pot, the safest thing you can do in the universe!"

After his well-delivered speech, Jack's collapse and sudden heart attack were a shock. He was rushed to the hospital and showed some progress when transferred to a rehabilitation center about a month later, but was unable to fully recover.

"The Hemperor" Jack Herer passed away on April 15, 2010, at the age of 70. He is survived by a worldwide circle of thousands of friends and fans.

Jack's life's work was a gift to all generations, creating the foundation of a more enlightened social consciousness, and an example of what one dedicated man can do when he puts his mind to it and his life into it. Jack's life's work was a gift to all generations, creating the foundation of a more enlightened social consciousness, and an example of what one dedicated man can do when he puts his mind to it and his life into it.

Jack the Ripper
TGAgenetics Subcool Seeds

J ack The Ripper is a product of TGA breeder Subcool's experiments in using outcrosses to boost the quality of backcrossed strains—in this case, blending a Space Queen male into a cubed backcrossing to work toward the original, F1 strain of Jacks Cleaner.

"The cool part is the outcrosses are sometimes better than the parent strains," says Subcool. "I feel this is the case with Jack the Ripper. The lemon tart of Jacks Cleaner has combined with the candy mango flavor of the Space Queen to create a resinous marvel." This cross is notable for its intense lemon smell, which while strong enough to discourage insects, does not really suggest pot—meaning that Jack the Ripper, like her fearsome namesake, might permanently evade the noses of the law.

Jack the Ripper's seeds are huge, and may require help shucking their hull. Once plants are started, they are hardy and easy to clone, making them suitable for first-time growers. Trifoliate seedlings, and two plants from one seed, are both common occurences. Jack the Ripper grows well outdoors in warm climates, or indoors in large bushes or SOG-style. When these plants are given moderate feeding and allowed to bush out, they finish in 8-9 weeks as a frost-covered miniature Christmas tree, just over 3 feet (1 m) tall. They may need an extra week or two of vegetative growth to compete with taller strains in a canopy.

JTR is a compact plant with dark, serrated leaves and tight colas attached to a study trunk. The plant's five to seven leaves can show pink veining if exposed to cool air, and may curl up around the third week of budding, like the leaves of a venus flytrap, as they become plastered with heavy resin. Indeed, growers will see very little green on this plant by harvest time; instead, she will be covered by an icy mantle of trichomes, like a dwarf spruce buried by winter. This promises a good yield of bubble hash or dry kief. Bud yields average 3-4 ounces (90-120 grams) per plant.

Jack the Ripper hits you behind the eyes with an almost lemon-cleaner palate and a jolting sativa buzz. About five minutes after this first rush, a long elation settles on the smoker, sometimes followed by munchies and drowsiness after a few hours. Anecdotally, medicinal users have reported an analgesic, almost body-numbing effect. Jack the Ripper has gotten many thank-yous for alleviating chronic pains. The mental side of the high leans toward happiness, chattiness, and trippy visual distortions, with potential for paranoia when indulged in heavily. Subcool notes that the lemon taste gets sweeter the longer these buds are cured.

 80/20

 speedy, trippy, talkative

 lemon

 56-63 days

 ♀ Jacks Cleaner 1985 SSSC (Nevil's) x ♂ Space Queen

 90-120 (3-4 oz.)/plant

 in southern climates

SOG

Jacky White ⚢

Paradise Seeds

Photos: Greenborn Identity

Like Jackie Brown, the working-class heroine created by Pam Grier and Quentin Tarantino, Jacky White is tough, fine looking, mellow, and pure woman—that is, her seeds are 100% female, an attractive feature for first-time growers who can be intimidated by the task of sexing the plants. Beginners will also appreciate Jacky's hardiness, high yield, fast finish, and striking profile; this is a truly aesthetically beautiful plant. This mostly sativa hybrid is also notable for her stability, with only slight variations between individual plants.

Outdoors, Jacky White likes a moderate to sunny climate. Indoors, hydro, coco, and soil are all excellent growing mediums. She likes to branch, so the garden setup that optimizes yield on these plants would allow a bit more space for the side branches to fully develop. Pruning or bending to increase yield works well with this strain.

 75/25

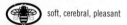 soft, cerebral, pleasant

 grapefruit

 60 days/mid-Oct.

 mostly sativa

 600 grams/m² in; 600/plant out

Jacky White smells like a grapefruit tree all through her flowering period, which finishes in 60 days at most, with an abundance of chunky colas glittering and luminescent with resin. Her indoor harvest is impressive—1 gram per watt of light per square meter, or up to 600g per square meter under a 600-watt high-pressure sodium light. Outside harvests are predictably larger.

Jacky White's growing style is sativa-like, with a note of good indica qualities (ease, hardiness, fast finish); likewise, her stone is sativa-like with a hint of indica to take off sativa's speedy edge. She offers a clear, mind-lofting cerebral high accompanied by a pleasant body buzz. Her stone has a smooth entry and exit that many will find inviting, with an enduring effect, although the rich haze-citrus taste may have tokers reloading their bongs anyway. Since she came on the scene in 2005, Jacky White has proven popular with German and Austrian connoisseurs. Like her cinema namesake, this attractive lady is likely to warrant attention that will move her into the big time.

Paradise's Feminised Seeds

Clones are a good alternative to feminised seeds. The production of feminised seed is not that easy, and has some pitfalls. Some of the feminised seeds available commercially partly turn hermaphrodite. The reason is that candidate plants are not carefully selected. Paradise Seeds uses only female plants that do not turn hermaphrodite even under stress. Then we treat this plant to induce the growth of stamins, which produce pollen. This pollen is then used to fertilize appropriate sister plants. This method is called "selfing," that is, crossing a plant to itself.

The seeds produced using this method will grow uniform superior female plants with abundant flowers. We believe that plants from seeds are much better than clones since they are stronger and more resilient.

Jilly Bean
TGAgenetics Subcool Seeds

Jilly Bean is the first strain bred by Green Avengers member MzJill. Her friend Charmed, another female grower, suggested the name. Like jelly beans, Jilly "Beans" are seeds that promise a sweet, fruit-flavored, happy-making treat.

Jilly Bean is easy to grow both indoors and out. When grown outside, this strain does best in dry, warm climates, where frost or rains don't occur until after mid-September. One fan of Jilly Bean has grown very successfully in Israel, using outdoor soil alone and no nutrients. Indoors, Jilly Bean adapts to either soil or hydro, and can be grown as a single-cola plant in SOG. She yields best as a large bush, topped several times, giving many large dense colas.

Jilly Bean has a light to average nutrient requirement. This strain is adaptable to higher grow room temperatures, but for maximum yields, the temperature should stay below 85°F when the lights are on. Jilly Bean will purple up if the dark time temperature is allowed to drop by 20 degrees or more, producing reddish or burgundy velvet leaves inherited from her Orange Velvet mother. Her leaves become darker and more leathery as she matures. The cooler the nighttime temperature, the more magnificent the hues of this lady will become.

Jilly Bean seeds express two phenotypes. One stays short and bushy with a lot of lateral branching. The other grows taller, with little lateral branching. When Jilly Bean is flowered between 24 and 32 inches in height, she finishes at approximately 4 feet (120 cm).

Jilly Bean buds grow in a pointy shape. They are dense and rock-hard from top to bottom, and forest-green in color, with some red hairs, and plenty of sticky resin. In good light and organic soil, this plant yields 3-4 ounces of primo sticky nugs. With an extra week of vegetative time, she can become even more robust. Grown in a hydroponic bubbler system, this plant can yield 10 or more ounces. It wafts the odor of sweet overripe mangos, pineapples, and oranges with a candied overtone. The pungency means it can be smelled from over a yard away, but doesn't have the classic "marijuana smell."

Her palate, too, is like pulpy citrus and candy, which makes her a tasty (as well as toasty) ingredient for cannabis bakers. Smokers will also enjoy the jellybean taste for its own sake. Her stone warms up slowly, speading evenly over mind and body. Mellow, giddy, and friendly, this is a good daytime smoke, and one that has been reported to alleviate chronic pain and depression.

 70/30

 creeper, mind/body relaxation

 mango candy

 56-63 days/early Sept.

 Orange Velvet – rare Pacific Northwest Orange Skunk clone♀ x Space Queen ♂

 90-120g (3-4 oz.)/plant; more in hydro

Drying and Curing Cannabis: The Art of Enhancing Effect and Flavor

By Franco
Green House Seed Company

Every cannabis gardener begins a new crop hoping to nurture healthy plants that deliver fat, tasty buds. Every crop involves months of hard work, from selecting varieties to vegetative growth, flowering, ripening, and harvesting. After all the effort, commitment, and waiting, the final stage

Freshly harvested bud with fan leaves trimmed off

arrives. It's too late to correct mistakes made during flowering, but it is never too late to improve the flavor and the high of your buds by implementing a controlled drying and curing process.

Drying for Success

Drying is as important as growing, and a bad drying process can ruin even the best buds. Drying marijuana means reducing the water content of the buds to 10-15%, depending on the desired crispiness of the final product. Most commercial growers do not cure their crop; they just dry it and sell it. Curing is a long but necessary step toward the highest possible quality of the smoke. For the real connoisseur, curing is the essence of it all, the culminating moment towards the perfect result.

There are many ways to cure and dry, but the method I like best is to use a climate-controlled room. The room should be lit using special green fluorescents or LEDs, because the green spectrum does not affect the plant material. The temperature and the humidity must be constantly controlled and adjusted, and the air exchange needs to be calibrated exactly to the desired volume.

In an ideal situation, most of the moisture should evaporate from the bud during the first three days, and then the drying process should be slowed. To achieve this rate of evaporation in the first three days, a temperature of 68° F (20° C) and a relative

Manicured bud ready for drying.   Photo: Subcool

humidity of 55% will ensure that the buds get to roughly 30-40% water content. From this moment on, the temperature should be dropped a few degrees down to 64° F (18° C) to slow the drying process. This allows the chlorophyll to decompose and the starches to be used up. If it dries too quickly more the chlorophyll will remain, and the smoke will be bitter and have a green aftertaste. The humidity of the air is also critical: If it drops below 50%, the buds will dry too fast. A timer

and heater/air conditioner system with humidity control will regulate air. In total, the drying process takes around 10 to 14 days for a perfect taste.

Taste is not the only variable affected by the drying process; the high is also affected. The longer the buds are dried, the more THC will degrade into CBN and other cannabinoids. Therefore even in the same strain, the effect will slightly change from higher to more stoned, from uplifting to more physical. The difference between drying 10 days

Buds Drying on hanging racks, save space and allow air to circulate. Photo: Justin McIvor

the flavor improves and the weed burns better. If the buds are to be smoked with tobacco, higher water content is preferable, up to 10-12% for good burning. When the weed is intended for vaporizing, it is best to leave even higher water content, 12 to 15%. This prevents easy combustion of smaller particles at vaporization temperature.

The Curing Process

After the drying is finished, the connoisseur will still dedicate a month or two to curing. Curing weed corresponds to aging a good wine. If the weed quality is average, it is not worth the effort and time necessary to cure it. On the other hand, if the buds are high grade, it is well worth waiting a little longer to get the best out of it.

I cure cannabis by packaging it in a wooden or cardboard box and pressing it slightly so that some of the trichomes break. Their oils and terpenes spread over the surface of the buds. After packaging, I leave the buds in an environment of 64° F (18° C), 50% relative humidity, and total darkness for a period of 1 to 2 months. Checking regularly ensures correct conditions. Make sure the humidity stays at 45-50% to prevent fungus and mold formation. If the buds smell moldy or like ammonia, the containers should be opened immediately, allowing the bud to dry in a warmer environment for a few hours before continuing the curing process. It is the result of curing undried plants.

Curing is an art and should be tried with small batches first. It increases the intensity of the flavor

and 14 days is not very evident to the novice, but creates a world of difference to the connoisseur.

After drying, gardeners package the crop. Commercial producers usually dry the buds to 15% water content; this results in a heavier product. (More water equals more money.) Connoisseurs like to use bud that has 80% water content because

Buds can not always be manicured when they are fresh. These buds are drying untrimmed, to be manicured later. Photo: Gracie Malley

and will slowly but steadily lower THC in favor of CBN, which is much less potent than THC. The high of cured weed is always deeper and more introspective, often becoming a meditation and inner-vision tool. The flavor becomes much more complex and refined, gaining in depth as well as in variation of bouquet.

Cured buds that were started a little moist look slightly brownish and have a typical deep smell, one that real smokers love from the bottom of their souls. Buds cured when they were dryer retain more THC, chlorophyll, and a fresher bouquet. Like very good aged wine, there is something unique about a well-cured crop that any aspiring connoisseur should experience at least once.

Kali Mist
Serious Seeds

Kali Mist was developed in the early 1990s, when many primo sativas from mysterious origins were gathered and selectively bred. Kali has had a series of fathers, creating slight differences based on time period. Seeds first sold under this name strongly resembled the typical Southeast Asian sativa, but an interim father in the 1990s gave the offspring a more Afghani look. With the new millennium, Kali's third father has returned it to a strongly sativa appearance.

Kali plants grow to a medium height with long internodes and medium-long fan leaves. The plant's structure is "open," meaning it's possible to see all the way through the space between the plants. This structure promotes good quality buds along the entire length of the stem because light can penetrate through the entire plant. Big individual flowers cluster closely together to form buds that are mostly leafless in 75 percent of the plants. The other quarter form a more traditional bud with many leaflets. On both types, glandular trichomes abound.

Seedlings are ready to flower after 30-40 days of vegetative growth, when they should be clipped to avoid ungainly heights. Clones are ready for flowering as soon as they are rooted, about 3-4 days. Indoor growing is recommended, by any method, including sea of green. Kali can be attempted outside where long growing seasons prevail.

With a sweet scent and flavor that spans both the sweet and spicy, this variety offers a cerebral high that leaves the mind clear and focused. Kali Mist's effects have proven beneficial for medical users with multiple sclerosis, fatigue and chronic pain. A popular choice among women, Kali Mist is a great all-day pot that can enhance energetic outdoor activities or more meditative, thoughtful pastimes.

1st place, *High Times* Cannabis Cup hydro division 1995
1st place, *High Times* Cannabis Cup sativa category 2000

 80/90

 cerebral, energetic

 sweet/spicy

 70-90 days

 2 sativa dominant hybrids

 SOG: 15-35g per plant in; 300-500g per plant out

 SOG

Kalichakra
Mandala Seeds

Kalichakra was named after the Hindu Godess Kali, the consort to the ganja smoking Lord Shiva famed for her omnipotent powers over life and death. This sativa prefers a warm, sunny climate when grown outdoors, but can also tolerate harsh weather due to her robust nature and resistance to mold. Kalichakra gives best results indoors when a minimum of 600 watts per square meter of light is provided. She also tolerates temperatures above the ideal.

Hydro and soil are equally good methods for this variety, but height must be monitored in a hydroponic system. Kalichakra, like many sativas, grows tall and will shoot up in a tremendously short time. The side shoots that develop at the internodes are vigorous, arching upward with little branching in between. Kalichakra's quality branch development make her an excellent candidate for motherhood.

When allowed to grow naturally, Kalichakra is a resinous, high yielding plant that disperses buds on all branches rather than concentrating flowering potential in one central cola. Her space conscious growth pattern allows her to be planted in close rows to maximize yield even in smaller spaces. Buds vary in shape: some are compact spheres, others are more stretched and airy.

Kalichakra has a potent and energizing body effect that awakens the Kundalini—the divine life-energy coiled like a snake at the base of the spine. It is a refreshing, strong stone for creative activities or social interaction. When indulged in heavily, this variety may cause a temporary bliss-out.

This strain has been used successfully for pain relief, and against depression. It is recommended for those seeking a long lasting high. Kalichakra exhumes a distinct spicy-fresh, herblike aroma when you rub the stems and flowers. The dried buds retain most of these aromatic qualities but are mild in taste and pleasantly smooth to smoke.

 alert, psychedelic

 mild spicy/fresh

 70-75 days indoors end Oct. outdoors

 ♀ Crystal Queen x ♂ White Satin

 500-600 g/m² (1½ - 2 oz./ft.²) dry weight

143

Kushage
TH Seeds

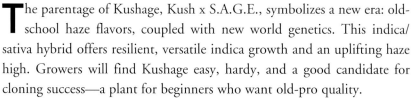

The parentage of Kushage, Kush x S.A.G.E., symbolizes a new era: old-school haze flavors, coupled with new world genetics. This indica/sativa hybrid offers resilient, versatile indica growth and an uplifting haze high. Growers will find Kushage easy, hardy, and a good candidate for cloning success—a plant for beginners who want old-pro quality.

This plant does amazingly well in places that are prone to powdery mildew. Just like her mother, she will be the last plant in the room to go down if left unwatered. When forced to flower at one foot (30 cm), Kushage will finish at 4.5 to 5 feet (140-160 cm). In sea of green gardens, plants deliver 25-40 grams (¾ to 1½ ounces) each. In one-gallon buckets, the yields per plant can increase up to 2 ounces (60 g). Larger plants in 5-gallon buckets produce 55-100 g (2-3½ ounces). When grown indoors, Kushage finishes in 10½ weeks. TH Seeds recommends hydro methods for biggest yield, or soil for the most succulent flavors. Like many mindful cultivators, TH Seeds recommends organic fertilizers for all gardeners.

Kushage starts off very straight, branches a lot, and tends to lean as she matures. It's a good idea to cut off the lower third of her branches to let the others breathe. Her first leaves are very wide, but subsequent leaves skinny up as the plant grows. They are waxy, and much darker than her buds, which are lime green, resembling her S.A.G.E. father. The large calyxes come from her Kush mother. Kushage buds are spade-shaped and frosty with fresh-smelling resin, giving the ripe colas a spiky or jewelry-like appearance.

If flowered soon after cloning, Kushage produces a single large cola with a rock-hard crown of lower buds. Kushage's buds retain their pine fresh scent as they dry and a spicy undertone that comes out when burned. This strain's sativa-dominant high is a great mind opener for brainstorms, conceptualizing, or creating artwork. It is less favorable when efficiency or punctuality is on the agenda. Medical patients have found this strain helpful for relieving the symptoms of multiple sclerosis.

3rd Prize, *High Times* Cannabis Cup (sativa category) 2005

 60/40

 quick, mind-expanding

 fresh, piney

 75 days

 OGer Kush from L.A. ♀ x S.A.G.E. ♂

 SOG: 25-40 g plantlets; 35-100 g/plant in

SOG

LA Confidential
DNA Genetics

Photos: Pistils

LA Confidential is a commercial seed strain that captures the genetics of OG Kush. An Afghan strain grown from clones, OG Kush first became popular in the Los Angeles market in the 1990s, and then became world famous as California rappers like Snoop Dogg, Method Man and Cypress Hill namechecked it in their songs. OG Kush offered a hash-like experience from reefer: a resinous smoke, deep and spicy-sweet like nutmeg, that drew the smoker into a lush, slightly trippy dreamland. While "Authentic OG Kush" may be hard to find if you're not a rap star, DNA's LA Confidential brings the secrets of this celebrity smoke to the market.

LA Confidential is an indoor-adapted plant that can also be grown outdoors or in a greenhouse. This strain is resistant to mildew, and on the whole is easy for even a novice to grow. She likes any medium—hydro, coco beds, soil, or NFT systems. If forced into flowering at 3-4 feet of growth (about 1m), LA Confidential stays petite, gaining only a foot (30cm) in the rest of her cycle, making her a good strain for gardeners with limited space. DNA themselves prefer bigger plants, vegetated for 3-4 weeks, for a lower overall plant count. Like many eco-conscious growers, DNA recommends organic nutrients.

As she moves through flowering, LA Confidential forms popcorn-like buds that are very dense, and so dark green that they almost appear black by harvest time. The flowering time is speedy, finishing in 7-8 weeks indoors, or by late September to early October when grown outside. These are the sweet "rocks" of resinous bud associated with her OG Kush ancestors. LA Confidential is not the biggest yielding strain, with average yields between 300-500 grams per square meter from "petite" plants in close quarters; yields from larger or outdoor plants may be correspondingly greater.

LA Confidential delivers a heavy "Kush" high: tasty, languorous, and a little psychedelic. Experienced smokers will find it relaxing but not sleepy, although probably too relaxing if there are complex tasks to be done. This is a chill-out smoke. What this strain lacks in monstrous yields it makes up for in high, taste, and smell. Many weed experts agree—LA Confidential has won second (2005) and third (2004) place for indica at the High Times Cannabis Cup, and first place for indica in the International Cannagraphics Cup (2005).

 100% indica

 strong and heavy but awake

 hash-like, spicy-sweet

 46-56 days/early Oct.

 California indica ♀ x Afghan indica ♂

 300-500 g/m²

 greenhouse

Léda Uno
KC Brains

Léda Uno acquired her mysterious Brazilian name directly from a South American woman named Léda who risked bringing male pollen from a Brazilian plant to KC in Holland. The pollen was dusted on a hybrid of Brazilian/Thai female crossed with KC 606.

Specially designed by KC Brains for outdoor gardening, Léda Uno should not be shied away from by indoor gardeners who prefer larger plants. Indoors or out, this lady likes arid weather and can stand very dry periods without difficulties. Moist weather may introduce problems, so consider the humidity levels and rain in the growing season of your region before committing to an outdoor grow with this variety. When grown in amenable European climates, a 3 month cycle from start to finish will produce a plant that is upwards of 12 feet (4.5 meters) tall, making this plant obvious to passersby if size is not controlled. However, a plant grown to this proportion can yield up to 2-3 kilos. Inside yields can vary between 20-100 g per plant under 400-600 watts of light, depending on the grower's method, ability and harvesting time.

A 60 percent sativa, Léda Uno is tall and sleek, with finger-like leaves and a sweet lemon aroma. The buds are fat indica-type colas. The taste is like a lemon drop, without the tangier tones that lemon sometimes evokes. While still growing, these plants exude a fresh aroma and appear sugar-coated with glands. The champagne of ganjas, Léda Uno can be bubbly and psychedelic, a sociable intelligent buzz. In greater amounts, however, she may leave you locked on the couch with your tongue tied and eyelids at half-mast.

2nd place, *High Life* Cannabis Cup 1998

 60/40

 body stone, giggly

 lemon citrus

 49-63 days in 77 days or mid-Sep out

 ♀Brazilian x Thai and KC 606 x Lédo Uno

 20-100g per plant in; 2-3 kilos per plant out

 out preferred

What Are Trichomes?

Prepared by Pistils
With thanks to contributions from Red Eyed Farmer and Snaps Provolone for the majority of the text and diagrams.

Cannabis resin glands are called "trichomes" These little lovelies begin to develop as soon as the plant starts growing, but the real explosion of trichomes comes during flowering.

Head on view of trichomes.

Why Did Trichomes Evolve in Nature?

Trichomes protect the plant, flower and especially the developing seeds from insects, animals, environmental conditions and diseases. The cannabinoids and various components of essential oils lend their protective qualities to these glands.

Insect Protection: Many insects find the thick sticky coating of trichomes unpleasant. Others get caught in the sticky trichomes. Some of the cannabis oils have repellent qualities to various herbivores. This offers a layer of protection from infestation by certain insects. It is especially useful for guarding the developing seeds.

Animals: The THC and other oils that make up the contents of trichomes have psychotropic effects that many mammals and other herbivores find unpleasant. This makes cannabis less palatable to many herbivores & omnivores. Fewer snackers means more chance of survival and reproduction. Desiccation: Trichomes help to 'insulate' the pistilate (female) flower from low humidity levels and high wind.

UV-B Light: UV-B light is a form of ultraviolet light that can be harmful to living things, THC has very high UV-B adsorption properties and more THC is produced in high UV-B light conditions. This implies that THC provides the plant with some protection from this harmful light.

Fungal and Bacterial Protection: Some of the oil components present in trichomes inhibit the growth of fungi and bacteria.

→ capitate stalked glands → capitate sessile glands
→ bulbous trichomes → cystolith hairs

Trichome Structures

While structurally diverse, trichomes tend to come in three basic variants.

Bulbous: The *bulbous* type is the smallest (15-30 micron) trichome style. One to four cells make up the "foot" and "stalk," and one to four cells make up the "head" of the gland. Head cells secrete a resin—cannabinoids and various terpenes which accumulate inside the balloon-like head cells. When the gland matures, a nipple-like protrusion may form on the membrane from the pressure of the accumulating resin. The bulbous glands are found scattered about the surfaces of the above-ground plant parts.

→ capitate stalked glands → capitate sessile glands
→ bulbous trichomes → cystolith hairs

Capitate-Sessile: The second type of gland is much larger and more numerous than the bulbous glands. These trichomes are called "capitate," which means having a globular-shaped head. On immature plants, the heads lie flush, appearing not to have a stalk. For this reason they are technically called "capitate-sessile." They actually have a stalk but it is only one cell high, so it is scarcely visible beneath the globular head. The head is usually composed of eight cells, but can be up to sixteen cells, and forms a convex rosette. These cells secrete cannabinoids and terpenes, which accumulate between the rosette and its outer membrane. This gives it a spherical shape. The gland measures from 25 to 100 micron across.

Capitate-Stalked: During flowering, the capitate glands that appear on the newly formed plant parts take on a third form. The "capitate stalked" gland consists of a tier of secretory disc cells which is topped by a large secretory cavity. Some of the glands are raised to a height of 150 to 500 micron when their stalks elongate.

Cannabinoids are found in greatest abundance in the "capitate-stalked" gland. These capitate-stalked glands form their densest cover on the female flower bracts during flowering. They are also highly concentrated on the small leaves that accompany the flowers. The male flowers have stalked glands on the sepals, but they are smaller and less concentrated than on the female bracts. Male flowers form a row of very large capitate glands along the opposite sides of the stamen.

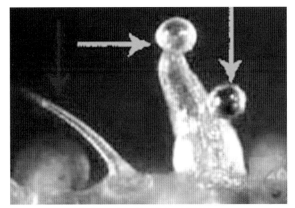

Magnification of glands along surface of leaf. Red-cystolith hair; green-capitate stalked gland heads, one of which has been decapitated.

Copious numbers of trichomes grow along leaf edge.

Life inside a capitate-stalked trichome
diagram by Red Eyed Farmer

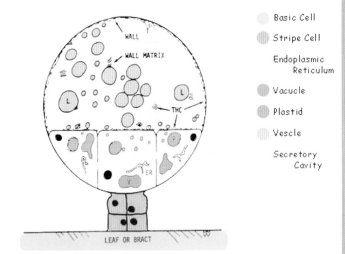

- Basic Cell
- Stripe Cell
- Endoplasmic Reticulum
- Vacucle
- Plastid
- Vescle
- Secretory Cavity

When to Harvest your Trichomes

There are several schools of thought as to the best time to harvest. I shall attempt to explain how you can determine the harvesting time that will produce the most favorable psychoactive effect for your individual preferences.

We are most concerned with the capitate-stalked trichomes, as these contain the overwhelming majority of the psychoactive cannabinoids, of which Delta-9 THC is the star.

Heavy trichome production is not necessarily an indication of a potent plant. Some hemp strains have moderate layers of trichomes yet only deliver a strong headache. In a recreational or medicinal marijuana strain, a thick layer of trichomes is the first indication that it may well possess an elevated potency level, but it is certainly not a guarantee. It is also necessary that those glistening glands are filled with potent THC.

A small 25x or stronger pocket microscope, which can be picked up inexpensively at an electronics store like Radio Shack or Maplins, works well for getting a closer peek at your trichome development. The goal is to examine the capitate-stalked glandular trichomes for the coloration of the gland heads, which varies between strains and with maturity. Most strains start with clear or slightly amber heads which gradually become cloudy or opaque when THC levels have peaked and are beginning to degrade. Regardless of the initial color of the secretory cavity, with careful observation you should be able to see a *change in coloration* as the bud ripens.

Red arrows indicate glands that remain clear, while yellow arrows show trichomes that have become cloudy and opaque.

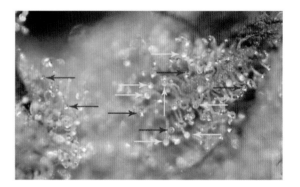

The diagram above denotes clear trichomes with red arrows, the yellow arrows mark cloudy trichomes, and the green arrows mark the amber trichomes.

Some cultivators wait for about half of the secretory cavities to turn opaque before harvesting, to ensure maximum THC levels in the finished product. Of course nothing tells the truth more than your own perception, so try samples at various stages to see what is best for you and the *phenotype* you are growing. While you may be increasing the total THC level in the bud by allowing half of the glands to go opaque, the bud will also have a larger percentage of THC breakdown products such as CBN, which is why some people choose to harvest earlier while most of the secretory cavities are still clear.

Indica varieties will usually have a 10-15 day harvest window to work with. Sativas and Indica/Sativa hybrids often have an extended period to work with.

Photo: Professor P, Dynasty Seeds

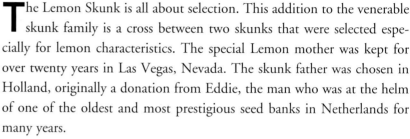

Lemon Skunk
DNA Genetics

The Lemon Skunk is all about selection. This addition to the venerable skunk family is a cross between two skunks that were selected especially for lemon characteristics. The special Lemon mother was kept for over twenty years in Las Vegas, Nevada. The skunk father was chosen in Holland, originally a donation from Eddie, the man who was at the helm of one of the oldest and most prestigious seed banks in Netherlands for many years.

The Lemon Skunk is a sativa-indica hybrid with a slightly higher sativa ratio. It has sativa-hybrid characteristics, growing tall but with a high calyx-to-leaf ratio, making it easy to trim. The structure of the plant tends to be open, but can get somewhat bushy, so it works best as a multi-branch plant. Lemon Skunk fares well with moderate to heavy nutrients and doesn't mind the heat. The leaves are a medium to lighter green with medium to slender sativa style leaflets, and the buds also stay light green and form a profusion of orange hairs. At finish, this bud is dewy with crystalline resin. The Lemon Skunk strain takes 8–9 weeks to finish, but reaches its apex of sweetness if cut down between 50 and 56 days.

Lemon Skunk is a tasty sweet citrus bud for those who like a fresh fruity stash. The enjoyable sativa-leaning high boosts the senses, bringing on thoughtful reflection and heightened sensory perception. It may also boost the sense for a need to go spelunk through the fridge for some munchies. Fans of the fresh-citrus end of the cannabis flavor palate will understand why Lemon Skunk has won multiple awards, including a cup at Spannabis and a first place win for outdoor at the Highlife in 2007.

1st place, Spannabis, Indoor Hydro category 2008
1st place, *Highlife* Cup Outdoor category 2007
2nd place, IC420 Breeders Cup 2008
Winner, *High Times* Top 10 Strains of the Year 2009

 60/40

 fast onset, energetic

 pungent, lemon

 56–63 days

 ♀ skunk x ♂ skunk

 400–500g per m²

Lowryder #2

High Bred Seeds

The long-awaited successor to the Joint Doctor's flagship strain is finally ready for your garden. Lowryder #2 is the newest development in High Bred Seed's quest to improve the strength, yield and flavor of the original Lowryder variety while maintaining the unusual characteristics that made this compact plant so popular.

Lowryder #2 is the second "dwarf" plant from Joint Doctor. This version is infused with superior Santa Maria genetics. The result is an auto-flowering dwarf that yields a wonderfully strong, head-turning sandalwood smoke with an earthy, rich taste. Besides strength and flavor, this strain boasts copious resin production and much-improved yield and stability. Her buds are larger, tighter and more aromatic than buds from the original strain of the same name.

This new cross was selectively inbred for three generations to ensure 100% auto-flowering, which derives from vestigial bits of Mexican-acclimated ruderalis genetics somewhere in her ancient history. Lowryder #2 is virtually "programmed" to begin flowering at 3 weeks, but the rapidity of her growth cycle can vary according to the intensity of light. As with the original Lowryder, no separate room or change of light cycle is needed to flower Lowryder #2. She finishes from seed to harvest in 2 months flat when given 14 hours of daylight per day.

Lowryder #2 branches a lot at the base, especially if topped at a young age. She responds well to moderate feedings, does not stretch, and seems particularly well adapted to indoor settings. Because Lowryder #2 does not require a long dark period in order to maintain flowering, she can be given up to 18 hours of light in the flowering phase, resulting in faster growth. This strain also matures faster than most non-auto-flowering varieties when grown outdoors in moderate climates. Although the breeder does not mention it, the autoflowering of this variety is due to a partial ruderalis ancestry. She is also suitable for temperate to Nordic climates and performs well in locations with short seasons.

Like the original Lowryder, this plant can be grown as bonsai cannabis. The average height of Lowryder #2 is 10-16 inches (25-40 cm), with yields around ½ ounce of resinous bud per plant. Her miniature size makes camouflage easy, while also allowing growers to garden in locations like window-boxes, patios, grow boxes, or closets, in addition to more standard garden setups. These plants do well as a sea of green.

Lowryder #2 has been dubbed "pot for dummies." This strain attracts many first-time growers because of her ease, speed, stealth, and stone: a strong and unusually uplifting indica high.

 mostly indica

 strong, uplifting

 sandalwood

 56 days (seed to harvest)

 Santa Maria x Lowryder (9th generation)

 ½ oz./plant

 SOG

LSD
Barney's Farm

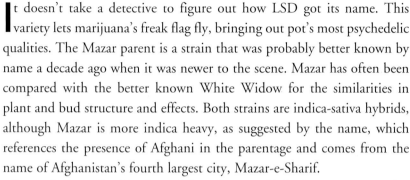

It doesn't take a detective to figure out how LSD got its name. This variety lets marijuana's freak flag fly, bringing out pot's most psychedelic qualities. The Mazar parent is a strain that was probably better known by name a decade ago when it was newer to the scene. Mazar has often been compared with the better known White Widow for the similarities in plant and bud structure and effects. Both strains are indica-sativa hybrids, although Mazar is more indica heavy, as suggested by the name, which references the presence of Afghani in the parentage and comes from the name of Afghanistan's fourth largest city, Mazar-e-Sharif.

Barney's Farm Seed Bank used these long established genetics in combination with the versatile Skunk #1 to create the LSD variety. These parents have passed along many of their strengths. LSD is a hardy, disease-resistant plant that thrives in nearly all reasonable growing conditions. These plants stay light to medium green with leaves that split the difference between

trippy, visual, euphoric

sweet, musky, earthy

55–65 days

Mazar x Skunk #1

600g per m²

in preferred

SOG

sativa and indica thickness. Flowering takes 8 to 9 weeks. At first the LSD plant may seem dense with foliage, but the buds soon outshine the vegetation. LSD buds form slightly curved corkscrew triangles with large stacked calyxes and a profusion of burnished hairs. While plants remain fairly compact and can be staked or grown successfully in a sea of green, LSD also delivers satisfying yields as a multi-branch plant, often reaching 600 grams per square meter. When grown outdoors, LSD plants finish in mid-September.

The LSD flavor mixes a slightly nutty and earthy palate with a dank sweet muskiness. Best of all, LSD lives up to its name, delivering a vivid, euphoric experience that stands out from the typical indica stone. While the body high has depth, the strongest sensation is the super trippy psychedelia that will blow the cobwebs out of the corners of your mind. This strain is great in a stimulating environment. Music, food, and colorful imagery will all be enhanced under its influence. However, overindulgence or overly hectic situations may cause a sense of being overwhelmed so it can be good to stay somewhere that also offers a sense of comfort and safety. Medical users have recommended this strain for nausea, anxiety, depression, and headaches. LSD won the 2008 Cannabis Cup in the Indica Category.

Mango
KC Brains

Mango's parentage is part KC 33 and part Mango from a hippie fellow who grew it for 30 years, then let KC use it as a cross in 1991. This variety is a 100 percent indica strain that grows large and produces prodigiously.

Don't let Mango's slow start fool you—this variety will eventually rival the impressive size of many KC varieties, which are especially intended for outdoor grows. If you want Mango to stay at an average size in an outdoor garden, allow only 3 weeks of vegetative time and transplant outdoors as late as July in Northern latitudes. Mango can also be grown in an indoor garden, but needs a lot of space. If you want some monster indoor plants, allow seedlings or clones to vegetate for 3-4 ½ weeks before changing to a 12/12 light regimen. Mango gardeners must rule with an iron fist if they want to manage the size of this plant, and it is important to start the discipline early. Accomplish this by starting the flowering phase about 1½ – 2 weeks after the seedling has sprouted and proven vigorous. Once established, Mango plants will grow so fast, you can practically watch them change height before your eyes.

Mango buds are massive and weighty, growing to lengths of 18 inches and the circumference of a woman's calf. Luckily the branches give sturdy support. As it matures, this plant's foliage can turn a very red to reddish purple color. The smell and taste are decidedly sweet mango and the stone is an even, mellow body sensation.

I

 body stone

 mango, sweet

 42-63 days in
63-77 days out

 Mango x KC 33

 4-5 kilos per plant

 out preferred

Photo: Gracie Malley

Master Kush
Nirvana Seed Bank

First called High-Rise, Master Kush was developed in one of the tall buildings of south Amsterdam. The coffeeshops instantly fell in love with this bud.

A vigorous plant, Master Kush thrives under most growing conditions, producing well in indoor and greenhouse set-ups. This variety grows into a medium-sized, compact, densely formed plant with sparse, spiky, forest green leaves. Master Kush's ball-shaped buds are light green with long hairs that range from white to orange in color. Buds are dense, thick, and heavy, which makes mold a risk in humid climates. Advantageously non-smelly while growing, the resulting bud has a hint of earthiness and sweet citrus but is virtually without taste.

Easy on lungs and palate, Master Kush is non-expansive and smooth to smoke, giving an all-over body buzz that is relaxing but awake. The high can also create optically pleasing effects, making it a good candidate for taking in a movie or museum visit.

Winner, *High Times* Cannabis Cup 1992
Winner, *High Times* Cannabis Cup 1993

 body stone, visual

 mildly earthly/citrus

 63-70 days in end Oct out

 Hindu Kush & Skunk sort

 varies

Photo: Nadim Sabella

Matanuska Tundra
Sagarmatha

Given to Sagarmatha from growers in the Matanuska Valley, this variety revives the majestic, legendary pot of the great Alaskan northland. This strain has also been known as Matanuska Thunderfuck, but Sagarmatha decided to use the more prudent "Tundra." As the Alaskan word for "grassland," Tundra makes this variety's name perfectly descriptive—it's grass from Alaska's grasslands!

Proven as a great stable breed for crossing, Matanuska Tundra has been widely used in Sagarmatha's hybrid programs. The flavor is chocolate, and the stone is a creeper, registering slowly and growing to a full, lethargic stone in the 5-10 minutes after a bong hit. Medical users have had good results alleviating pain with this variety.

An indica with enormous, palm-like leaves, Tundra stays short, but grows very thick with numerous side branches. Fat colas are coated with a frosty glacier of THC crystals. Sagarmatha recommends growing indoors. In an arid outdoor environment, this variety produces some chunky pot bushes that stay close to the ground and give good yields.

Gardeners should gauge Matanuska Tundra's ripeness by the lower portion of the buds because the tips of the top buds will keep growing when the rest of the bud is ripe. Waiting for the tips to finish can cause frustrating and unnecessary delays in harvesting. Sagarmatha breeders experimented with this phenomenon, waiting to harvest one plant until the tips finished.

After 115 days, they surrendered even though the top buds still had new, immature white hairs when they harvested. This plant must also be dried thoroughly because it may mold during the drying period if all of the moisture is not able to escape.

 creepy, sleppy

 chocolate

 60-68 days in Oct out

 Alaskan hybrid

 350-375g per m² in

 in preferred

Mazar
Dutch Passion

 80/20

 body stone

 earthy/soft pine

 56-63 days
early-mid Nov.
outdoors

 ♀Afghan x
♂Skunk #1

 400 g/m² (11/3 oz./
ft²) SOG indoors
300 g (10 oz.) per
plant outdoors

 SOG

Named for the cannabis growing center in Afghanistan, Mazar-I-Shariff, this variety derives from a resinous indica descended from marijuana's motherlands, and a Skunk #1 mother that adds some of her sweet sativa traits. This plant does well outdoors in the welcoming climates of Spain or California, but her November finish at Holland's latitude encourages an indoor setup. Mazar also makes a good greenhouse plant.

Growing vigorously in either soil or hydro, Mazar tends toward a squat dwarf-conifer silhouette, a meter (3 feet) tall or less, that suits sea of green cultivation. She carries long chunky colas and thick leaves that stay green over her whole cycle. A third flowering wave comes just before harvest, so growers that are able and willing to let her continue growing may be rewarded with additional yields.

An unobtrusive pine and sandalwood aroma makes Mazar easy to conceal, and easier on the lungs and palate than other hashy varieties. This inhale full of soft incense is a quick ticket to turning up the Technicolor of psychedelic enjoyment, but may also lead to couch-lock and even heavy sleep. Smokers are slow to build up a tolerance to Mazar so this strain can be reliable as a nightcap. The occasional Mazar expresses sativa phenotypes, including a more upbeat and heady stone. Mazar won second prize in both the 1999 *High Times* and the 2002 *High Life* contests.

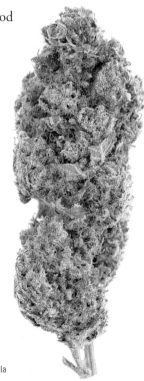

Photo: Nadim Sabella

Medicine Man

Mr. Nice Seed Bank

A proven medical marvel, Medicine Man is ideal for those in need of high THC levels. This variety has a strong heritage stemming from the Brazilian and South Indian genetics of White Widow crossed with a prodigious yielding Afghani. Sibling to the award-winning White Rhino, Medicine Man is indica in appearance, with a sturdy Christmas tree formation and immense crystal production.

Buds are dense and solid with yellow and red hairs. This variety changes color to silver as it finishes. Those who prefer to grow indoors can expect an incredibly resinous, compact plant. Outdoor gardeners will find that Medicine Man can get large outside and will get even stronger resin under natural sunlight. Medicine Man is not the easiest plant to get right but with love and attention, presents no real problems for the dedicated gardener. Mr. Nice Seed Bank recommends fertilizing conservatively for optimal results.

A proven champion for sick and terminally ill patients, the aptly named Medicine Man is serious stuff. Due to its heavy, sedating effect, you want to monitor your intake while toking, and especially when eating it in baked goods. This very strong, long-lasting buzz has proven effective for many conditions that benefit from cannabis, including anorexia, glaucoma, severe headaches, depression, AIDS and cancer/chemotherapy.

 body stone

 acrid, ripe fruit

 56-60 days in Sep to Oct out

 Brazilian sativa x South Indian x Afghani

 up to 600g per m²

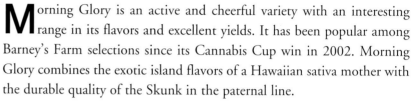

Morning Glory is an active and cheerful variety with an interesting range in its flavors and excellent yields. It has been popular among Barney's Farm selections since its Cannabis Cup win in 2002. Morning Glory combines the exotic island flavors of a Hawaiian sativa mother with the durable quality of the Skunk in the paternal line.

Skunk varieties are known as versatile plants that contribute many desirable and durable qualities to more delicate and challenging strains. Sativas are generally known to be lankier and more finicky in the garden, and this can often be a greater concern with varieties adapted to specific locales. Hawaiian varieties, like other island-acclimated strains, may lose their special Polynesian flavors and vibe when moved to more temperate locations. In Morning Glory, the Hawaiian mother has been infused with skunk genetics, adding a hardy efficiency to its growth. Yet the surprisingly subtle earthy floral flavors of the Skunk also allow the island qualities to drive the flavors and effects.

Morning Glory plants are somewhat branchy, working best when branches are retained rather than pruned to a single-stem plant. This plant's growing structure is truly hybrid, with medium leaves and a medium growing height and structure. Barney's Farm recommends growing Morning Glory in soil with organics. Plants finish in early October outdoors, or in 8–10 weeks of flowering indoors, with average yields of 450 grams per square meter.

In their natural state, Morning Glory buds have a distinctly strong, citrus aroma, but the smoke is mild and just a bit earthy and spicy, with subtle hints of almonds and white pepper. The high is soaring yet simultaneously relaxing. It can enhance energetic or social activities, making it a true "morning glory," yet it serves equally well when more sedentary or passive activities are planned, whether laying on the beach or simply watching a summer movie.

 60/40

 cheerful, thoughtful

 nutty, grapefruit, spice

 65–70 days

 ♀ Hawaiian sativa x ♂ Skunk II

 50–100g/plant in 200–500 g/plant out

Starting Seeds Right

By Ed Rosenthal

A seed is the distillation of a plant's essence. It contains the blueprint for life, which it holds in storage until it senses environmental conditions favoring survival of a new plant.

Once it's made contact with the requisite amount of moisture and proper range of warmth, the seed starts the process of germination. A cascade of chemical reactions results in the rapid growth of the embryo plant, which had been kept in suspended animation.

Marijuana germinates best at room temperature, around 72° F in a consistently moist environment. The first visible sign that a seed is germinating is a slight enlargement resulting from water absorption. Then a small opening appears along the seed's seam as the root emerges. The root continues to elongate, growing downward, as the stem makes its appearance. It stretches out in the opposite direction of the root and uncurls, revealing two embryonic leaves called cotyledons. The seed case is now an empty shell and it may hang from one of the cotyledons until blown or rubbed off. Only a day or so has elapsed between the first sight of the root and the appearance of the cotyledons.

In its first phase of growth the seedling used energy stored in the seed, but it must soon use photosynthesis to produce its own food as its roots supply moisture and nutrients The root grows longer and lateral branches grow from the vertically growing tap root. The first set of true leaves emerge at the tip or apex of the stem, which is called the apical tip.

Healthy germination is an auspicious start for a successful plant. When the plant's needs are met, the seedling will grow and prosper. Growers use different methods of germinating seed.

Germination methods:

Soak the seeds in a solution of water with commercial rooting solution and hydrogen peroxide (H202) for 12 hours. The hormones in the rooting solution stimulate germination and encourage root growth. Use rooting solution according to instructions

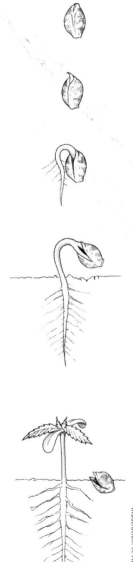

Illustration: K. Abellán

for softwood cuttings and add hydrogen peroxide at the rate of one part to 200 (.5%) to sterilize the solution, preventing infection. Drugstore peroxide is a 3% solution; if it's used, add it at the rate of one part H202 to five parts water. Compost tea can also be used as a soaking solution to create a biologically active community around the seed.

After soaking you can place the seed between

a thin wet cloth or paper towel on a plate with a clear cover or plastic wrap. When the root emerges, plant it by first poking a hole in the planting mix that is long enough for the entire root area to be covered. Then gently place the seed and pat it so the root makes contact with the medium. The other method is to plant the soaked seed into the medium before it germinates. Place it ¼ inch deep in sterile commercial planting mix. Moisten the mix with water adjusted to a pH of around 6. Keep it in a bright space with high moisture. If the space is dry, place a tall cover over the container to reduce evaporation. Keep at room temperature. If the air is cool, use an electrical tray warmer and cover.

Stretching:

The main problem that people encounter when germinating is stretching seedlings. This is an indication of insufficient light intensity. To encourage strong, stout stems that don't stretch, seedlings must be provided with intense light from the start. -a minimum of 40-60 watts per square foot (400-600 watts per square meter). With a bit of care quality seeds will be sprouting in just a few days.

Motavation
Magus Genetics

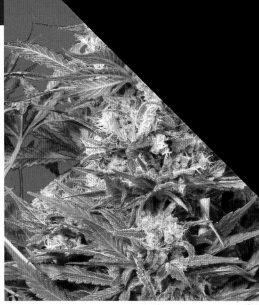

Motavation may seem like an ironic name for this highly relaxing couch-lock strain, but the quality it calls to mind, one stoners are stereotyped for lacking, is not its origin. It is instead named for a favorite band of the Magus Genetics crew, a band who named themselves for mota, the Spanish word for pot. This strong indica will "mota-vate" smokers to put up their feet and take it easy for a while.

This strain's indica/sativa mix can only be estimated since both parents have an uncertain or "top secret" ancestry, but Motavation's stone and appearance confirm her indica-dominant genetics. Short and squat, this plant is a little leafy and shows moderate stretching at flowering. The copious resin on her leafy matter may put you in the mind to become more earth friendly and "recycle."

This indoor plant is best suited as a multi-branch grower. Her lateral growth is strong, sometimes even equalling growth on the main stem. Sea of green cultivation is also possible, using a short vegetative time. When vegetated for 4-5 weeks, plants will reach approximately 2½ feet (80 cm) and yield about 80 grams apiece.

Motavation buds will mostly be firm but not rock hard. Her leaves are a thick, dark green. A reddish purple coloration often emerges at the end of the flowering cycle, especially when plants have been exposed to low temperatures. As with most plants, her yield is reduced if low temperatures have been the norm throughout the cycle.

Motavation's odor is strong and penetrating with a touch of petrochemical, like turpentine or fresh paint. The flavor is much softer and richer, a strong complexity of carbon and sweetness like sweet tobacco or raisins. The high starts in the head, as your thoughts wander off, soon followed by a deeply relaxing but not necessarily soporific body stone. The reduction of tension may be just what some people need to drift off, but even if it doesn't make your eyes droop, it is not really a sensible "day smoke" choice. This variety may leave you couch-locked and lost in your own thoughts. While it may awaken some interesting connections and inspire you, it is unlikely that you will be motivated to act on them until the mota has worn off.

 30/70

 quick head high/ physical, possible couchlock

 carbon, sweetness

 50-60 days

 Sensi Star, M.I., Holland ♀/ Warlock, M.I., Holland ♂

 80 g/plant

 less desirable

Nebula
Paradise Seeds

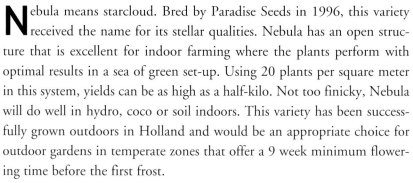

Nebula means starcloud. Bred by Paradise Seeds in 1996, this variety received the name for its stellar qualities. Nebula has an open structure that is excellent for indoor farming where the plants perform with optimal results in a sea of green set-up. Using 20 plants per square meter in this system, yields can be as high as a half-kilo. Not too finicky, Nebula will do well in hydro, coco or soil indoors. This variety has been successfully grown outdoors in Holland and would be an appropriate choice for outdoor gardens in temperate zones that offer a 9 week minimum flowering time before the first frost.

Nebula stretches slightly, but produces obesely fat buds when placed under lots of light. Like the name suggests, Nebula twinkles with the coating of THC glands, which are bound to take you into the realms of space—or possibly just make you spacy. The buzz is transcendental and cerebral, sometimes bordering on the psychedelic. Nebula may earn the nickname "honey pot" for it's sweet smell and distinctively honeyed fruit flavor. This variety is a fun tasty smoke, even for the veteran stoner.

4th place, *High Times* Cannabis Cup 1999
4th place, *High Times* Cannabis Cup 2000

 cerebral, trippy

 fruity, sweet

 60-65 days

 White Widow & potent father

 SOG up to 500 g per m² in; 500-600 g per plant out

Nevil's Haze

Green House Seed Co.

Named for the breeder who began this hybrid, Nevil's Haze is a mostly Haze sativa that was crossed to be one-quarter indica. The Haze variety is renowned for being a tall gal, and Nevil's version follows it's genetically programmed desire to seek the sun by outgrowing its competitors.

Nevil's Haze leaves are very thin and long, with sparse buds and long internodes. This strain has a pine cone smell with a distinctively floral haze edge. The resin is abundant and the high is very potent and cerebral, encouraging a spiritual or philosophical disposition. With a THC content of 11 percent, Nevil's Haze can also induce a kick-in-the-pants, psychedelic type of buzz. CBD has been tested at 1.2 percent and CBN present at .1 percent.

Recommended as an indoor plant, this is a variety for those with the patience to wait the full 10 weeks required for a proper finish. Gardeners can skip the vegetative growth cycle and go straight to a 12/12 light schedule. This serves to control the height, and can also compensate somewhat for the long flowering time. Hydroponic methods are preferred indoors, but soil can also be workable. Forget growing this outdoors if you aren't within 20 degrees latitude of the equator. Nevil's Haze needs that long season of intense sun, and will be hard pressed to finish outside in most parts of the world. A real connoisseur plant, Nevil's Haze resists stressors well as long as tropics conditions are met.

Winner, *High Times* Cannabis Cup 1998

 75/25

 psychedelic

 pine, floral

 98-100 days in out at equator

 Haze x mystery indica

 medium to low

 in preferred

New York City Diesel
Soma's Sacred Seeds

Soma's New York City Diesel is a pungent sativa with incredible yields. Soma added some Hawaiian and Afghan indica influence to the popular, almost purely sativa Sour Diesel. This raises the hybrid's calyx quotient – NYC Diesel becomes a colossus of airy bud formation with very few leaves. Soma reports indoor yields of up to 100 grams per plant with some extra vegging. The strain favors indoor cultivation except in tropical climates, although good yields have been reported in the semi-arid climate of Southern California.

This strain can reach 12 feet (4 meters) outdoors or 3½ feet (150 centimeters) indoors. Soma reports best indoor results from growing NYC Diesel as a multi-branch plant in guano-fertilized soil. The plant responds well to heavy cropping, which encourages it to form four or five big top colas. NYC Diesel's few leaves are thick and wide—more palm than finger—and dark green turning more purple toward harvest. A bed or garden of these tall conifer-like ladies smells exhilarating, like a grove of ripe grapefruit. "Tart citrus" also defines their taste, a little sweeter than the mother strain's lemon tang.

Soon after the exhale, bygones will become bygones and clouds of obsessive hard feelings will be broken up by rays of sweet creative energy. NYC Diesel is a cerebral daytime toke with a hint of body stone, good for recreation and making or enjoying art. This strain has placed in three Cannabis Cups and is a popular café smoke in Amsterdam.

 60/40

 uplifting, creative, smooth

 ruby grapefruit

 70 days indoors
beg. Nov. outdoors

 ♀ Sour Diesel x
♂ Afghani-Hawaiian

 30-100 g (1-3 oz.) per
plant indoors
500-3000 g (1-6 lbs.)
per plant outdoors

Northern Lights

Sensi Seed Bank

The Northern Lights (NL) is one of the most potent and famous indica varieties. Even though there are a lot of copies circulating around with variations on the name, there are only 3 pure types from the original development of Northern Lights, which Sensi was lucky to acquire.

Historically, the NL 1, a longer, more stretchy type with a fresh scent and good bud formation, was the basis of the NL cross that was sold as Sensi's Northern Lights. Currently, the NL 5 has taken over the most important role in the cross. Because NL 5 adds potency and reduces flowering time, but is not dominant in taste and smell, it also plays a starring role in the overall breeding plan at the Cannabis Castle. It has functioned as a test case for many crosses. The F1 generation is very predictable, giving uniform results and passing uniformity on to the hybrids it parents. The NL 2 contributes to the overall vigor of the plant and strength of the high, also lending its spider mite resistance to the cross.

Highly adapted to indoor growing, Northern Lights is a satisfying yielder that can finish in just over 6 weeks. The best results are obtained from hydro culture gardens. Small sea of green plants or bigger indoor plants will both do well, but remember that yield is directly related to the amount of light and space.

A petite plant averaging between 3½-5 feet (110-150 cm), NL has dense, resin-rich flowers and wide-fingered indica leaves. The aroma is pungently sweet and the taste is a flavorful mixture of sweet and spicy. The high is a potent physical experience that feels comfortably lazy and relaxing.

Northern Light's fame extends to the harvest festivals where it claimed the overall *High Times* Cannabis Cup win in 1990, and the Cup's award for the pure Indica category in 1988-89.

I

narcotic, body high

sweet, pungent, spicy

45-50 days

Northern Lights 5 x Northern Lights 2

450g per m²

SOG

Northern Lights Haze
Sensi Seed Bank

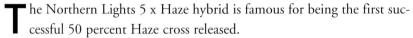

The Northern Lights 5 x Haze hybrid is famous for being the first successful 50 percent Haze cross released.

The Haze is a long (up to 6 months) flowering sativa from the U.S. Very popular in the 1970s, it became nearly extinct in the late 1980s because growers were switching to easier, higher-yielding varieties. Breeders at the Cannabis Castle crossed Haze genetics with the uniform and quick-finishing NL 5 indica to make a lush producer with a refreshing high.

Due to the radically sativa nature of the Haze, this cross stretches a lot and takes a longer flowering period to finish than most common cannabis hybrids. This stretchy quality also allows cuttings to enter flowering as soon as they are rooted. Some growers even start the seeds under a 12-hour light regimen with success. This early entry into flowering phase allows NL-Haze to finish in a similar amount of time as conventional, indica-heavy crosses that need more vegetative time. The growth tendencies of the NL-Haze are enhanced when grown as larger plants and diminished in a sea of green method.

Don't be tempted to harvest too early. Long flowering crosses can create some nail-biting for the grower, but tenacity and some experience pay off with buds of superb quality. NL-Haze delivers fresh, spicy sativa-type buds that have a clean, peppery taste. An immediate, cerebral high, this pot has sometimes been referred to as "speed weed" in Holland. Overall NL-Haze is a friendly high with a trippy edge that adds some extra zing to any day.

Winner, *High Times* Cannabis Cup overall 1994
Winner, *High Times* Cannabis Cup mostly sativa category 1990 and 1994

 up, psychedelic

 fresh, peppery

 65-75 days

 Northern Lights 5 x Haze

 380g per m²

 SOG

NYPD (New York Power Diesel)

Nirvana Seed Bank

The New York Power Diesel (NYPD) is an indoor power strain with a radical mix of Sativa Mexicana father and Afghan/Dutch indica mama. The Nirvana addition to the diesel family stays close to the New York variant. NYPD is an F1 hybrid that is balanced but sativa-dominant, with potential for gardeners and home breeders. Its mother plant, the Aurora Indica is a combination of Northern Lights and an Afghan strain that was stabilized especially for use in this cross. The heavy, greasy narcotic effects of the Aurora Indica beautifully cut the edge of the crispy, speedy Oaxacan sativa father known as Eldorado. The resulting terpenoids have a powerful diesel aroma with a lemon-edged fuel flavor.

NYPD grows tall because the sativa influence creates moderate spacing in the internodes and long stems. The branches are lanky but sturdy and are neither spare nor profuse, allowing the grower to decide which direction to take the gardening setup. Soil and organics maximize the aromas, but these plants are pretty dank and smelly in the grow space regardless. The dark green calyxes form chains of big popcorn buds that are surprisingly tight in structure. Hairs turn red toward maturity. NYPD yields are good—in a sea of green with 600-watt lights, gardeners can expect between 350 and 450 grams per square meter.

The New York Power Diesel is a blissful, balanced, and relaxing buzz that makes great campfire joints. It is a treat to smoke, starting with a clear, enjoyable transition and bringing a mixture of earthiness and lemon zing, over a recognizable deep note of diesel acridity. This buzz brings out a sense of calm, wonder, and sensory awareness. It can enhance discernment and pleasures. NYPD makes one notice the subtle flavors of foods, the enjoyment of the smells, sights, and sounds of the outdoors, and has potential as an aphrodisiac.

 70/30

 soaring, clear, relaxing

 lemon & earthy fuel

 65 days

 ♀ Aurora Indica x ♂ Eldorado

 350–450g per m²

Orange Bud
Dutch Passion

 80/20

 up, active

 orange goodness

 55-65 days indoors
end Oct. outdoors

 Skunks

 20-25 g (¾-1 oz.) per
plant (SOG) indoors
200-250 g (7-9 oz.) per
plant outdoors

Orange Bud expresses the sativa-leaning qualities from its family of vigorous growing skunk ancestors. A fast, cooperative plant, this variety grows well indoors or out, in any system or medium. It is suitable as a multi-branch plant but yields best in a sea of green. The minimal foliage makes pruning optional. Outdoors, Orange Bud flourishes in Southern Europe and other similar climates. When autumn's chill approaches, her outdoor leaves turn purple, setting off the orange pistils that cover her buds—a beautiful plant.

After 30 days of vegetative growth, Orange Bud will be about 2 feet (60 centimeters) tall. Every additional week of growth will give approximately 7 inches (20 centimeters) of extra height, reaching a meter (3 feet) around harvest time indoors, or 2 meters (6 feet) outdoors. Orange Bud's leaves are classic seven-pointers. Her branches are long, and can be weighed down by the grape-like buds that grow at different sites along their length, making staking a good idea.

Orange Bud pot leaves a citrus note on the tongue, tending toward the sweet and floral like a very ripe orange or a tangerine. By the time the taste registers on the tongue, the buzz is palpable. Orange Bud is an uplifting, active mental stone, compatible with any activity. Its fast onset makes it attractive for medical relief from nausea and obsessive, distracting thoughts.

Pineapple Punch
Flying Dutchmen

Photo: Cannabis College

The Flying Dutchmen's popular Real McCoy strain crosses a Hawaiian indica with Skunk #1. Real McCoy is backcrossed with its Skunk parent to produce Pineapple Punch. Interestingly, this hybrid expresses two distinct phenotypes. One is a more "sativa" pattern—tall and rangy with thin leaves and widely spaced internodes; the other is a more "indica" growth pattern, with medium-size, wider leaves, closer nodes and a slightly stronger bouquet and yield. Growers will know by the vegetative phase which trait package to expect from their plants. Both phenotypes produce the citrus taste and cerebral, active stone of their Real McCoy mother.

Outdoors, Pineapple Punch grows fairly tall with lime-colored leaves, large bracts and golden pistils. Indoors, the Dutchmen recommend growing Pineapple Punch from clones either at 12-16 plants per square meter (1-2 per square foot) unpruned or at 6-9 per square meter (1 plant per square foot), pruned once. Removing lower branches channels light and energy to the tops of the plants. Flying Dutchmen prefers soil cultivation with a 12/12 light-cycle and low to medium regimen of organic nutrients, but hydro cultivation is acceptable, too. No nutrients should be applied for at least 10 days before harvest.

Pineapple Punch's buds are medium-dense and loaded with sugary fruity resin. Her high terpene levels preserve her inviting taste and smell after water extraction, although dry sieving gives the best results. While both phenotypes offer a smooth pineapple/grapefruit smoke, the "sativas" have a sweet lavender undertone while the "indicas" are stronger and more grapefruit-astringent.

Pineapple Punch's tropical spell is likely to leave you giddy. This is a great upbeat high that brings on talkativeness and lots of grinning. A terrific accompaniment to an outdoor concert or a walk in nature, Pineapple Punch encourages a sunny perspective and offers a pick-me-up for recreational afternoons.

 70/30

 motivational, talkative, smiley

 lavender, pineapple

 63-70 days indoors end Oct. / beg. Nov. outdoors

 ♀ Real McCoy x ♂ Skunk#1

 300-500 g/m² (1-1½ oz./ft.²)

 SOG

Power Plant

Dutch Passion

Power Plant derives from dagga, the sativa-dominant pot grown in South Africa and its neighboring countries. South African varieties are famous for their fast growth and early finish, in contrast to the slow growing season required by most tropical sativas. Power Plant develops almost visibly, finishing before Halloween outdoors in the Netherlands and even sooner in semi-arid, Mediterranean climates like Spain. This is a plant for growers who want strong sativa, ASAP.

Flexible and adaptive, Power Plant grows well indoors, whether in soil or hydro, multi-branched or in a sea of green. If pruned, she develops multiple compact buds that measure around 15 centimeters (6 inches) long. If she isn't pruned she grows three or four big 20-centimeter (8-inch) buds and lots of smaller popcorn. Power Plant's foliage stays olive green with thin, seven-point leaves. Her strong, pungent smell may require odor control in regions where inconspicuousness is a must. She prefers an easy hand with fertilization, and her rapid growth is very uniform: plants finish at an even 70 cm indoors (just over 2 feet), or 100 cm (3 feet) outdoors.

This power sativa's smoke tastes sharp and lights up the neural networks after a few hits. Many sativa highs can be sustained during a serious working day, but Power Plant may prove too strong for work settings. Instead, she's rocket fuel for a launch at 4:20 p.m. or later. With an uplifting, mostly mental high, Power Plant is quite compatible with dinner and freewheeling conversation; however, many sativa fans will also enjoy tripping out with a few tokes of this variety and a sketchbook or an interactive game.

 80/20

 up, giddy, playful

 pungent, sandalwood, pepper

 56-63 days indoors 49-56 days or end Oct. outdoors

 South African parents

 0.75-1 g per watt indoors 150-400 g (5-14 oz.) per plant outdoors

 SOG

Querkle

TGAgenetics Subcool Seeds

Photo: Subcool. Plants in photos were grown by Dioxide

The name "Querkle" is a clever twist on this indica-dominant strain's heritage. The mother strain is the Purple Urkle, a memorable Pacific Northwest variety that is easily recognized for her super short stature, slow growth pattern, and amazing transformation in late flowering to a lavender goddess reeking of grapes and purple goodness. In a linguistic mash up of the parentage, Querkle takes its "Q" from the male Space Queen used in this breeding line. Space Queen is one of Subcool's breeding projects that combines the well-known BC strain, Romulan, and the famed Cindy99 from the Brothers Grimm. The breeding male of Space Queen, nicknamed "Space Dude," is good for adding speed and stretch to most crosses.

Querkle has wide leathery leaves and a typical short, thick indica profile. It thrives indoors or outdoors in climates that have good weather until late October. These moderate feeding plants have almost no stretch, so they can be vegetated longer in order to gain size. Even though they stay compact, Querkle's internodes are tight. Breeder Subcool recommends topping them early. It is also a good idea to thin out the fat lower fan leaves to allow light to reach the lower branches. Once topped, Querkle plants form large three-headed bushes with bottom stems as big around as your thumb. When given sufficient vegetative time, topped, and grown in soil, plants consistently yield 4 ounces each.

A sea of green method can also be used. Clones that are budded at 12 inches (30cm) produce about ¾ ounce (21g) per bud site. These plants also do very well when untopped and grown in a screen of green style. Beginners and advanced growers all seem to enjoy growing Querkle. Fans of color will be thrilled by this plant's transformation as it flowers. The undersides of the fan leaves turn the rich reds of burgundy wine midway through flowering. As they reach maturity, the leaves and stems become dark purple, and the entire plant takes on a purplish-silvery black shading. Buds are dense and heavy with a purple tint.

Querkle is mostly a nightcap smoke, and may encourage late night snacking. It can also be a nice companion for hikes or other mellow outdoor activities. The buzz comes on slowly and lasts a long time. The sensational flavors are worth cleaning out the pipe or bong so they can be thoroughly savored. This strain's primo taste and the gradual buzz may take discipline to avoid the heavy zoned stone of overindulgence. Querkle is also a good choice for making tinctures, which are calming and very helpful with sleep disorders or nighttime leg pain.

 80/20

 calming, sedative, munchies

 musty grapes, fruit, berries

 63 days

 ♀ Purple Urkel x ♂ Space Queen

 135g per plant

 in preferred

 SOG

SAGE
TH Seeds

SAGE stands for Sativa Afghani Genetic Equilibrium, but also describes the aroma of this interesting hybrid. SAGE's mother is a native Californian called Big Sur Holy, a sativa with a long finishing time but strong mold and bug resistance. She is combined here with a chunky Afghani indica selected for its extreme characteristics—hardiness, tight internodal structure, and fast finishing time—and grown from seed for cross breeding.

The vigorous growth, elegant leaves, straight growth pattern, and hefty weight of the Afghani balance with the pleasant, mentally alert and thoughtful sativa high, which continues to be satisfying with repeated use. A fulfilling equilibrium of the parental lines, this plant deals well with challenging conditions, and will usually be the last plant standing in a stressed garden. SAGE holds her color and resists mite infestation.

The SAGE flavor is "old-school," reminiscent of the days when Colombian and Thai stick were still primo. The aroma is like the wild sage native to the sativa mama's California homeland. This fresh smell is also a helpful factor for the stealth grower—the odor doesn't readily give away its source. Even without charcoal filters, trained noses may not recognize the scent as weed.

SAGE responds well to topping and is also amenable to the bend technique because the branches hold the rubbery quality of the Afghani papa. This plant likes to grow large, so it works great in beds as a larger plant but is too wily for a sea of green method. Hash made from this variety won first place in the 1999 Cannabis Cup and scientific analysis by an unaffiliated testing facility reported that SAGE's THC content is over 20 percent, ranking in the top 3 varieties tested.

 cerebral. alert

 woodsy, fresh

 70-85 days

 Big Sur Holy x Afghani indica

 300-350g per m²

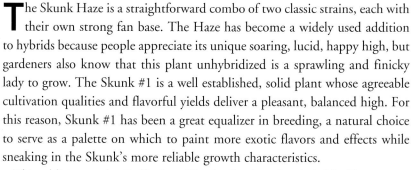

Skunk Haze

Coffeeshop Classics by Ceres Seeds

The Skunk Haze is a straightforward combo of two classic strains, each with their own strong fan base. The Haze has become a widely used addition to hybrids because people appreciate its unique soaring, lucid, happy high, but gardeners also know that this plant unhybridized is a sprawling and finicky lady to grow. The Skunk #1 is a well established, solid plant whose agreeable cultivation qualities and flavorful yields deliver a pleasant, balanced high. For this reason, Skunk #1 has been a great equalizer in breeding, a natural choice to serve as a palette on which to paint more exotic flavors and effects while sneaking in the Skunk's more reliable growth characteristics.

This addition to the Coffeeshop Classics line is truly a hybrid of its parents. It has retained the lanky, willowing branches of the Haze. At maturity, the buds make the branches top heavy and are best supported by netting or in a screen of green garden. The Skunk's influence diminishes the stretchiness, reduces the time spent in flowering, and creates a denser cola, leading to a more manageable beginner-friendly plant.

At finish, Skunk Haze is taller than the average hybrid, a happy medium between the typical Skunk and the typical Haze. The open structure is a swooping inverted triangle with light, fresh green tones and slender sativa leaflets. The buds stay pale green and form orange hairs. Because the Skunk Haze balances indica and sativa qualities, the buds aren't too compact and resist mold well. In fact, this plant likes a moist environment and thrives in a garden that mimics the tropics in heat and humidity. Keeping the humidity low will bring out more of the skunk qualities. Outside of equatorial locales, this variety makes a better indoor grow. The open structured qualities of the Skunk Haze also make it a whole lot smellier than the typical indica or hybrid.

Beginning cultivators with a yen for haze, or a general sativa-leaning will be satisfied with this variety. While growing, the haze smell is dominant, but when breaking buds, the Skunk's florid tones will be evident. Both are truly carried through in the flavor, which tickles the nose with fruity haze, but leaves an undertone of musk and earth from the Skunk lingering on the palate.

The Skunk Haze is primarily a head buzz with a lingering body stone that carries through. When plants are harvested after two months of flowering, the cannabinoid/THC balance tends to deliver a more mental high and fluffier buds. At 70 days, the buds become denser, and the increased CBD creates a stonier effect reminiscent of Jack Flash. It is always possible to progressively harvest in order to find the best balance. Overall, this variety has an energetic and clear headed yet leisurely effect that is anxiety-reducing and low on paranoia.

 55/45

 energetic, leisurely

 fruity haze, earthy

 70 days

 ♀Haze x ♂Skunk #1

 1g per watt

Strawberry Cough
Dutch Passion

 80/20

 happy medium

 strawberry

 56-63 days

 unknown

 15-25 g (½ -1 oz.) per plant

Strawberry Cough is a sweet-flavored indoor variety with just enough indica influence to shorten the typically slow growing time of the semitropical sativa into a two-month flowering cycle. The creamy berry taste combines with its expansive smoke to deliver a variety worthy of its name.

Strawberry Cough gardens efficiently whether using hydroponics or soil setups. It is too branchy for sea of green, but Dutch Passion recommends planting 15-20 plants per square meter (1-2 plants per square foot). Strawberry Cough likes a boost of nutrients at the beginning of vegetative growth. Although no data was available for outdoor gardens, Strawberry Cough performs terrifically in greenhouses.

Strawberry Cough is a plant of happy mediums, growing to a height of around 3 feet indoors or in a greenhouse garden and exhibiting leaves that balance between indica and sativa influences. This multi-branched plant will start delivering ripe colas about 40 days into flowering, and continue with a second wave that finishes at about 65 days. Greenhouse flowering times are typically a week shorter than indoor gardens.

The buds are tight and shaped like narrow pinecones, and may get quite long. This variety's branches are sturdy and support even the weightiest of colas. Strawberry Cough tickles the lungs with her creamy-sweet smoke, whose flavor resembles strawberry, perhaps with a kiwi fruit complement. The buzz is heady and active, a classic let's-go-hiking sativa lift that can alleviate depression.

Photo: Nadim Sabella

♀♀ (Arjan's) Strawberry Haze

Green House Seed Company

Photo: Jan Otsen

Arjan's Strawberry Haze is a bright green mid-sized sweet sativa. She descends from Swiss stock on her mother's side, and popular Northern Lights and Mist varieties on the paternal side. These seeds are feminized, meaning that they will all grow out as bud-producing female plants. The Strawberry Haze's buds have the aroma of an almost candy-like strawberry, and her smoke is sweet-tasting with an upbeat high.

This mountain plant is adapted to humid areas, and overall very versatile, strong, and easy to grow. She ranges from 3 feet in small containers, to 10 feet when her roots are given free reign. She has short internodes and medium-sized round leaves. Her branches tend to shoot out vertically, straight toward the light, allowing plants to be placed closer together than is possible with more rangy sativas. Three to four plants per square meter is an ideal arrangement.

Strawberry Haze performs best and delivers the utmost in strawberry flavor when grown in soil. Hydro systems can be used to increase the yield, but the taste is less sweet. Green House recommends a light hand when it comes to nutrients, as this plant is more sensitive to overfeeding than most sativas. Start with a low pH (5.6 hydro / 5.8 soil) and slowly increase to reach 6.5 at the end of flowering. Extra P and K should be added after the 5th week of flowering. The maximum EC should be 1.9 in hydro and 1.7 in soil. Flush plants at the end of flowering, which takes about 10-11 weeks or until mid-October outside.

Arjan's Strawberry Haze finishes with chubby buds, composed of rounded calyxes that are thickly coated with resin and thin long hairs. Aside from the expected, very sweet strawberry aroma, which is much sweeter than most sativas, the smell has also been compared to summer blossoms, rose petals and red berries. Her high is fast hitting, clear, creative and giggly. It is good for social moments as well as for introspective ones. Chasing the blues away, making love, making friends laugh, and making art are all recommended activities to accompany this strain. Arjan's Strawberry Haze was created by Arjan in the period 2000-2004. He introduced it on the market in 2006, after winning the 1st prize among Green House's strains at their Very Important Smokers Panel event in 2005.

 70/30

 clear, creative, giggles

 strawberry

 75 days/mid-Oct.

 Swiss sativa ♀/ NL5 x Haze-Mist ♂

 500-600g/m² in; 800g/plant out

 below 45°N latitudes

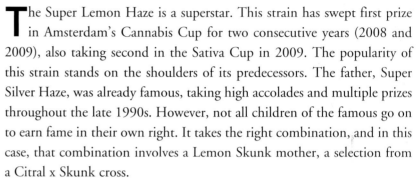

Super Lemon Haze

Green House Seed Company

The Super Lemon Haze is a superstar. This strain has swept first prize in Amsterdam's Cannabis Cup for two consecutive years (2008 and 2009), also taking second in the Sativa Cup in 2009. The popularity of this strain stands on the shoulders of its predecessors. The father, Super Silver Haze, was already famous, taking high accolades and multiple prizes throughout the late 1990s. However, not all children of the famous go on to earn fame in their own right. It takes the right combination, and in this case, that combination involves a Lemon Skunk mother, a selection from a Citral x Skunk cross.

The Lemon Skunk mother brings a fragrant lemon intensity to tantalize haze fans, as well as adding steady skunk genetics that will appeal to growers. The haze influences still make this a better multi-branch plant. Super Lemon Haze retains a willowy sativa growth pattern and forms long buds bearded in extra long hairs. This variety does equally well in soil or hydro and prefers a high PK intake in later flowering. Although Super Lemon Haze can technically be grown both indoors and out, it is limited to the region between 40 degrees latitude North and South outdoors. It is faster and more forgiving than its haze papa, but most Super Lemon Haze growers will be gardening in the great indoors. At finish, Super Lemon Haze averages 3.5 feet indoors, but may get up to 10 feet tall in the proper outdoor setting.

The winning combination of lemon/lime pungency and strong spicy haze background is undeniably delectable. The Super Lemon Haze taste is a citrus fruity bite with a light acridity. Haze flavors of musky-woodsy earth resonate in the undertones. Flavor aside, sativa fans will really go gaga for the obvious qualities that make Hazes so well loved. The high begins with a strong and immediate physical sensation, followed by a soaring cerebral sense of elation. This pot has a fizzy social side, bringing people out of themselves into a good humored, giggly and vivacious mood. Super Lemon Haze is not for serious or heavy introspection, nor is it well suited to solitary tasks that require a single-track focus. Although it can range into the slightly dreamy, this is definitely an active, clear, and emotionally uplifting buzz that is best suited to recreational activities. Medicinally, it has been reported as good for appetite stimulation and nausea.

euphoric, intense, electric

acrid fruity, musky-woodsy haze

63–70 days

Lemon Skunk x Super Silver Haze

100–200g per plant in
750–1000g per plant out

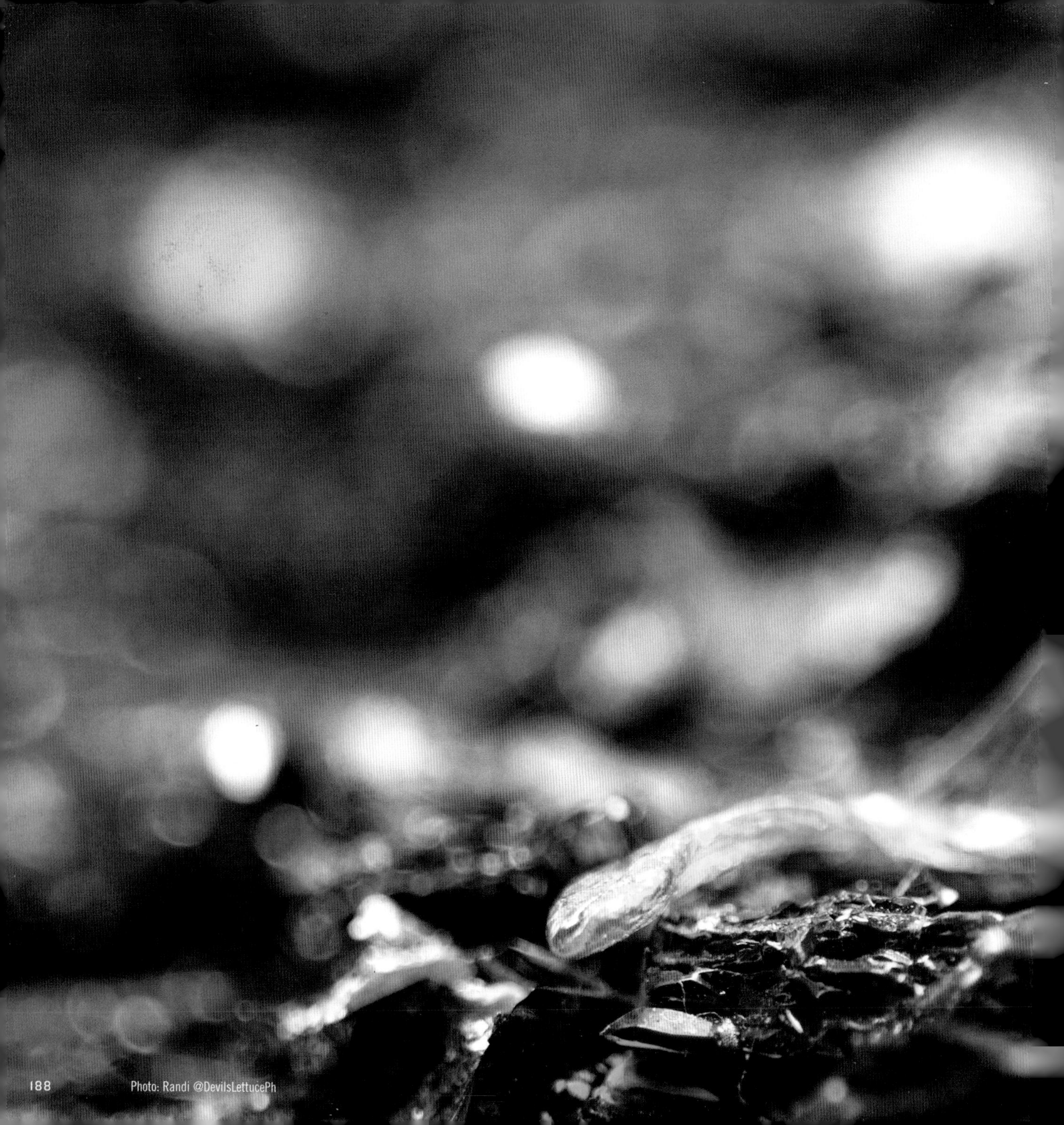

Photo: Randi @DevilsLettucePh

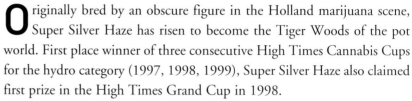

Super Silver Haze

Green House Seed Co.

Originally bred by an obscure figure in the Holland marijuana scene, Super Silver Haze has risen to become the Tiger Woods of the pot world. First place winner of three consecutive High Times Cannabis Cups for the hydro category (1997, 1998, 1999), Super Silver Haze also claimed first prize in the High Times Grand Cup in 1998.

Super Silver combines the stellar genetics of three super plants—the Skunk, Northern Lights and Haze varieties—to deliver an all-around good indoor grower. This variety can also be grown outside in the equatorial zone, approximately between 35 degrees latitude North and South. While she is best grown hydroponically, Super Silver Haze has not let her stardom go to her head. She will produce highly resinous and strongly pungent flowers in most indoor growing set-ups. The colas get pointed on top when mature, and are more open than compact, which makes them harder to manicure but well worth the effort. Sea of green is only recommended for those growers who are masterful at controlling height, since the Haze influence gives this strain a tendency to shoot up.

This variety has a complex nose: a combination of the floral Haze with the sweetness of the Skunk and deep Afghani undertones from the Northern Lights. The flavor is pungent and spicy. Super Silver Haze has a buzz that covers the complete spectrum of effects, with a full-body stone and esoteric, philosophical attributes, making this highly rewarded pot a stash for all seasons.

1st place, *High Times* Hydro Cup 1997, 1998, 1999
1st place, *High Times* Grand Cup 1998

 even head-body

 pungent

 56-63 days in late Oct out

 Skunk, Northern Lights & Haze

Tahoe Gold
Master Thai Organics

Tahoe Gold is a 50/50 sativa/indica hybrid that mixes four classic "heirloom" strains of 1970s landrace cannabis. The mother is the sativa side, a tall airy stinky-sweet bush that combines a 1975 Thai strain grown from seed with a circa 1976–1977 Skunk #1. The indica father is a cross of a 1974 Hindu Kush and a 1977 variety from Afghanistan.

This agreeable plant was bred at high altitude—just over 7,000 feet, so it fares well at low to high altitudes. Tahoe Gold grows well in any method or setup, but particularly likes coco coir and guano fertilizers. These plants spread out as they branch, but they tend to form one big fat bud on the main stem, making them suitable for a sea of green grow. Tahoe Gold plants start slowly, gaining speed as they progress, and loading on weight during the last two weeks of flowering. Plants need at least 9 weeks after flower forcing. Impatient harvesters who pluck their buds before a full 63 days will significantly decrease the yield. Outdoor flowering times are a little longer, typically about 10–11 weeks, finishing in the second half of October.

These balanced hybrids form wide pine trees with serrated medium leaves and rock hard colas. Tahoe Gold is good for both beginning growers and more experienced gardeners after a connoisseur harvest. Because these are responsive and resilient plants, they can help the beginner learn gardening basics and graduate from cannabis cultivation 101 with a completed garden of connoisseur yields. Indoor plants finish at about 6–7 feet (3 meters) and have per-plant average yields around 3.5 ounces (100g), but outdoor plants may get as tall as 10–12 feet (4 meters) and produce a whopping 4 pounds apiece (~2kg).

The Tahoe Gold variety gets its name from the attractive red-gold hues of the finished buds. These colas hearken back to the 1970s when varieties such as Panama Red or Acapulco Gold were top shelf, even though this strain's parentage derives from other geographic regions. These buds have an interesting, gilded appearance and a blissful and balanced high. Tahoe Gold invites a relaxing state of body and mind. Its functional buzz gradually takes effect, like sailing on a gentle breeze. It invites a playful and positive attitude. The smell and flavors are tropical and sweet, like a pungent berry candy. When made into hash or cooked into food, this variety can make the eyes very heavy and affect one's balance. The breeder of Tahoe Gold is a medical user with permanent nerve damage, and this is his pot of choice for pain management. Others with chronic pain conditions may also find this strain offers effective pain relief in combination with a lucid and awake state of mind and a happy attitude.

 50/50

 blissful, functional, happy

 pungent tropical berry

 55–65 days

 ♀Thai/Skunk #1 x ♂Afghan/Hindu

 112–450g per plant in 1500g per plant out

 SOG

The Church

Green House Seed Company

Photos: Jan Otsen

The L.A.-based heavy metal band, System of a Down, sat in with Green House breeders on a little variety naming session back in 2005 when they appeared on the Very Important Smokers panel. They helped Green House to arrive at the name "The Church" after the lyrics in one of their songs.

This mostly indica variety is suitable in temperate and mountainous environments as well as balmy regions more conducive to outdoor grows. She is particularly well suited for areas with high levels of humidity due to her extraordinary mold resistance. Indoors, this plant performs best in soil-based gardens, although she also does well in hydroponic systems. The Church is a rugged, adaptable plant that branches moderately to form a rounded bush of modest height. Her mid-sized internodes are more extended than most indicas. Green House recommends spacing these plants at one per 2 square feet to allow each one to fulfill her potential. Pruning might also be in order to direct the plant's energy into her most valuable branches.

The Church can soak nutrients, especially in hydro setups. The pH should be started at 5.6/5.8 and slowly increased to 6.5 at the end of flowering. The maximum EC should be 2.1 in hydro and 1.8 in soil. Plants require 9 weeks to ripen and should be flushed in the last weeks to ensure the best quality and flavor.

This plant flushes to purple rather quickly if exposed to low night temperatures. Her mature buds are replete with thick short hairs. The Church's round clustered nuggets of bud take on a sage-like sheen due to the silver-gray tone of the resin.

The predominant sensation on first smoking The Church is mental stimulation and ease, followed by a steady descent into the body, which feels clean and loose-limbed for many hours afterwards. Tastewise, spring flowers and red berries keep the flavor light and sweet. Rather than the jolt of heavy-hitting strains, The Church offers a mild, progressive high that doesn't rule out work, play or socializing.

 70/30

 mind/body

 floral, berry

 63 days

 Swiss Sativa Skunk ♀ x Super Skunk/ Northern Lights ♂

 700-800 g/m² in; 900g/plant out

What is the SCREEN OF GREEN (SCROG) Growing Method?

By Franco
Green House Seed Company

Photos: courtesy Sannie's Seeds

The SCROG system is the practical application of a very simple concept: a screen, or net, is placed horizontally over the plants during vegetative growth, and the plants themselves are allowed to stretch through the screen toward the light. The screen can be used in several ways. Sometimes branches are tied to the screen to form a flat surface under the lights. At other times the screen simply serves a support function for the vertically stretching branches and later for the buds. The benefits for the grower derive from the versatility of the system. The height at which the screen is placed depends on many factors, including the desired crop height, the plants' genetic predisposition to height, and the intended length of the vegetative growth period. The screen is usually made of nylon netting or a rigid grid, and it has open squares ranging in size from 4 to 12 inches (10-30 cm). The larger the openings, the less support the plants will get. On average, SCROG demands less plants per square meter compared to SOG, and it is especially useful for a setup in which only a few large branchy plants are being grown in a confined space.

SCROG in a Grow-Box Setup

When the SCROG is applied in a grow-box context, it is usually to flatten the canopy and to form

SCROG keeps each bud growing straight up, within its own section of the canopy.

A rigid frame was placed over these plants to spread out the branches.

a solid, well supported layer of flowers, one that can be kept at the desired distance from the lamps without risk of overstretch and burning. When approaching SCROG in a grow-box, it is important to consider a few determining factors: the heat threat, the absence of light under the screen, and the different needs in plant nutrition that this system requires.

Heat is always an issue in a grow-box system. The reality is that most grow-box producers for the commercial market are more concerned with security and discretion than with plant health and well being. As a result, most grow-box systems lack proper ventilation in favor of a quiet, stealthy setup. When SCROG is applied to a confined space, it is important to realize that there will be two completely different climate areas inside the grow-box: an "over-the-screen" climate and an "under-the-screen" climate. The temperature over the screen will be much higher, and that's where

Looking up at the screen.

the hot air should be vigorously pumped out on a constant-flow basis. Fresh air should be pulled in from under the screen, so that it travels through the canopy to reach the exhaust fan.

Another issue to monitor is the near-absence of light under the screen. It is recommended to trim any small branches and leaves that don't receive enough light so that they stay green and healthy. Getting rid of these weak, penalized parts of the plants will improve the general well being of the canopy, thus reducing stress and increasing production.

Finally, the feeding needs of the plants have to be considered. When plants grow long and stretchy side branches, they benefit from extra N and P during the first weeks of flowering. This is especially important when growing sativas. Moreover, longer branches and a hot canopy demand more water and will need water at shorter intervals. The size of containers has to be large enough to allow plants to grow into and over the screen without sacrificing the pace of new growth.

Other SCROG Set-ups

Screen of green can also be successfully applied to very different situations, such as growing really tall plants indoors. When vertical space is not an issue, maximal production is achieved by exploiting the height of the plants. This is particularly true when growing sativas. In order to grow very tall plants without the problem of branches bending during heavy cola formation, a single or multiple SCROG can be applied. In a multiple SCROG, plants are allowed to grow through more than one layer of screen so that they are supported at different set heights. Usually 2 or 3 screens do the job. They are placed at 1- to 2-foot (30-60 cm) intervals. The plants grow through the screens, and when they reach the top screen they are tightened to form a flat canopy. This system requires additional lateral light since the stages of growth between the first and last screens have to receive adequate light to avoid stress and lack of productivity.

Whether using one screen or multiple screens, once the system is in place and the plants are growing through a screen, it should n[...] again. This means that the growroom [...] set up to allow watering and maintenance wi[...] any need for moving or altering the screen pos[...] tion. If the screen covers a large area, an automatic watering system is usually the best option, unless the plants are very tall and the screen is placed high enough that walking under it is possible. As for the grow-box setup, it is convenient to trim the lower branches since they cannot receive good light.

Overall, SCROG is not a system that can, or should, be viewed as static. The only stationary part is the position of the screen itself. All other factors must be flexible to guarantee the best results. SCROG should be seen as a way to improve an already tested growroom or grow-box. If, for example, one tries to grow really tall sativas, but has falling branches and broken buds as a result, SCROG is a good solution. Besides being inexpensive, easy to use, and easy to dismantle, SCROG is always a fun experiment. At harvest, the screen can be recycled as a plant hanger during the drying process, a true expression of its flexible nature.

Netting was stretched across a wide area in this greenhouse to support the buds as they grew through it.

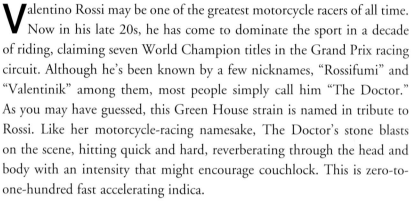

Valentino Rossi may be one of the greatest motorcycle racers of all time. Now in his late 20s, he has come to dominate the sport in a decade of riding, claiming seven World Champion titles in the Grand Prix racing circuit. Although he's been known by a few nicknames, "Rossifumi" and "Valentinik" among them, most people simply call him "The Doctor." As you may have guessed, this Green House strain is named in tribute to Rossi. Like her motorcycle-racing namesake, The Doctor's stone blasts on the scene, hitting quick and hard, reverberating through the head and body with an intensity that might encourage couchlock. This is zero-to-one-hundred fast accelerating indica.

A champion producer, this mostly indica variety generates the heaviest, most dense bud of Green House Seed's collection. Besides being a powerhouse of production and stone, The Doctor is also an easy-to-grow plant that performs well for beginners and experienced growers alike. Soil-based setups will deliver sweeter tastes, but hydro delivers a bigger yield. Outdoors, this variety matures properly in temperate and Mediterranean zones as well as in subtropical regions, finishing around the end of September in the Northern hemisphere.

The Doctor is a bushy, indica-dominant plant that requires trimming to clear away her lower branches, and prefers 2 square feet of space per plant. This variety enjoys generous feedings, especially in hydroponics systems. Green House recommends adding extra phosphorus and potassium about midway through flowering, in week 4, in order to maximize flower development. EC levels should not exceed 2.4 in hydro and 2.0 in soil.

The buds on this plant may remind you of primitive totems peeping out of a jungle. Massive colas jut out from the fat dark green leaves, looking oddly out of proportion to the short bushy stature of the plant. Rounded calyxes shoot in all directions from the cola profile. The flavor is sweet, earthy indica with a skunky background.

 80/20

 fast, intense head/body

 pungent sweet

 56 days

 Great White Shark x South Indian ♀ x Super Skunk ♂

 700-800 g/m² in; up to 1200g/plant out

The Kali
Big Buddha Seeds

Kali, the dark and fierce Hindu goddess, is a powerful force, bringing change. In the yin-yang of Eastern cultures, this goddess is both destructive and creative, nurturing and protecting her children, but also defending them with violent ferocity. In Tantric beliefs, Kali is a dominating force, foremost among the goddesses. Her name in Tantra expands to also mean the original form of all things, or ultimate reality. Kali is usually portrayed as a many-armed dark-skinned blue or black goddess with glittering eyes and a fearsome extended tongue.

The strain known as "The Kali" originates from the Afghani/Pakistani border. It is a landrace OG Kush that was selfed with a reversed Kali clone father taken from seeds whose male was responsible for the original backcross that led to the Cup-winning Big Buddha Cheese. Kali is from old-school indica parents, the real hashmaking deal from the home of ancient hashmaking tradition, an area that has selected for hash excellence among its plants over generations upon generations.

The Kali is a dark fierce-growing indica that has thin dark green leaflets and very little but very sturdy branching, especially for such an indica-influenced plant. She likes moderate to heavy feeding and will do well in any substrate from soil or coco to hydro. The Kali is not a large plant, usually entering flower at 2 feet (70 cm) and finishing between 4–6 feet (1.3–2 meters). The Kali stands up well to heat or cold and is good for growers at all levels of experience. The yields on this plant are good indoors or out, with each plant easily delivering a kilogram (2.2 pounds) if treated with respect. The buds are conical and as resinous as you'd expect from a hash-derived variety.

The Kali has a dark hash smell in the garden and throws out buds like fat feathered goddess tongues. The buds glisten with rich layers of THC, the dense ambrosia of this goddess plant. Kali is an obvious choice for hashmaking. Cured buds will also have a very hashish-like flavor and aroma, dense and smooth, with a unique, earthy citrus-kush richness. This is slow trajectory pot, with a flow of euphoria and creeper body stoniness. The Kali is the manifestation of Kundalini energy, which is one's dormant energy force that lies at the base of the spine and, when awoken, restores vitality. Kali brings awakening in her dark tasty form, and her delights will make her a savored addition to any collection.

 80/20

 sedative, stoney, intense

 lemon-lime, kush

 56–70 days

 ♂♀ OG landrace

 500g per m² in 1000g per m² out

 SOG

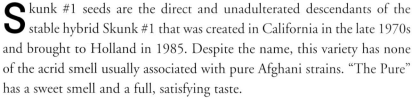
Skunk #1 seeds are the direct and unadulterated descendants of the stable hybrid Skunk #1 that was created in California in the late 1970s and brought to Holland in 1985. Despite the name, this variety has none of the acrid smell usually associated with pure Afghani strains. "The Pure" has a sweet smell and a full, satisfying taste.

Skunk #1 is a 75 percent sativa with a modified sativa appearance—it stays shorter than most sativas with leaves that are few and large, and short internodes. The big flowers range in color from lime green to gold at harvest. Although the buds are dense, they allow enough airflow to avoid mold problems. Resistance to molds makes The Pure a perfect variety for greenhouse cultivation where high-quality, heavy dense buds and uniformity are essential. The Afghani parent speeds up the finishing time to 8 weeks indoors.

Flying Dutchmen regularly yields 500 grams per square meter when growing this variety in a greenhouse in soil. They recommend using all-organic medium and fertilizer for the highest quality results. This strain offers all the flavor and the clear, cerebral effects of a sativa with the quick maturation of an indica. The Pure Skunk #1 was awarded the very first *High Times* Cannabis Cup in 1987.

 75/25

 cerebral

 sweet

 56 days in; Oct out

 ♀ Mexican Colombian x ♂ Afghani

 up to 500 per m²

Flying Dutchmen on the Skunk #1

Back in the 1960s, the scene in Holland was more hashish than pot, as the available grass was mostly mediocre imported stuff. By the mid-1970s, a small number of Dutch enthusiasts started growing at home. The first strains were large plants with small buds of average taste and high, but a few seeds eventually made it over from Afghanistan. Then this weird character from the States showed up with some new varieties: pure breeding strains from Colombia, Afghanistan and South Africa. More importantly, he brought over a few crosses he had made himself, including the Skunk #1, earning him the nickname, "The Skunk Man."

The Skunk #1 was a Colombian/Mexican/ Afghani cross. Flying Dutchmen breeder, Eddy, was one of the main enthusiasts in the growing scene at the time, and while initially skeptical about the Skunk Man's claims, he decided to grow out this guy's seeds and let the results speak for themselves. Eddy used the greenhouse method of simulated day and night cycles that predated the current indoor growing revolution. In 1984, the first crop was grown out and the results were so astounding, Eddy knew he'd found the future of Dutch weed, and never looked back.

Eddy says that the Skunk #1 was the first true stabilized hybrid in Holland's marijuana world, changing the trajectory of cannabis in the Netherlands. According to him, the initial selection was more fundamental than the breeding in making the Skunk #1 what it is. The combination of Afghani and sativa genetics brought together the best of both worlds.

The one conundrum remains this variety's widely known name—contrary to expectation, the taste is delicate, more floral than anything, and completely lacking the pungent tones that the word "skunk" evokes. Flying Dutchmen has employed the pure strains of the Skunk Man in many varieties, using other strains he introduced as mother plants and a hybridized Skunk #1 as the father. The original Skunk #1 line is also made available as "The Pure," in appreciation of the Skunk Man's contribution to the evolution of breeding.

The Purps
BC Bud Depot

This scrumptious purple plant comes out of Mendocino County, in northern California, where she began as a clone-only plant among the medical marijuana community. BC Bud Depot has developed a stable cross to make Purps seeds available. The Purps is a good in indoor and outdoor environments, finishing well in a coastal British Columbia climate.

The Purps is a pungent girl with medium thick leaves and green hues that turn more purple as the plant ripens. Her moderate side branching makes her amenable to both pruning for a sea of green garden, and, alternatively, encouraging her to spread out as a multi-branch plant. BC Bud Depot prefers growing The Purps in soil with medium organic feedings, because it enhances the flavors in this smooth and complex strain—hints of buttery caramel coffee and woodsy floral pine.

Indoors, The Purps reaches an average 3-4 feet (around 1 m) at harvest, while outdoors she can grow to 6 or 8 feet (2-2.6 m). Her height can be controlled by shortening the vegetative phase, which may also influence her final crop. The Purps's indoor yields range from 1.5 to 2.5 ounces (40-70g) per plant, while outdoor plants will produce 4-5 ounces (120-150 g) each. These plants require 8-9 weeks to finish, which places harvest in the last half of October. Although she is a hardy, pest-resistant strain, the Purps is more suited for gardeners with a few crops under their belts.

The buds are tasty looking and smelling, with deep purple coloring and a frosting of resin. The flavors are soothing and tantalizing, lingering pleasurably on the tongue. The Purps high soars into a longlasting purple haze of playful euphoria. It produces an active, awake feeling with a very low burnout factor. A nice antidote to depression, these rich flavored buds turn the blues to the Purps.

 60/40

 giggly, blissful

 caramel, coffee, earthy

 56-63 days/late Oct.

 Mendo "Purps" clone only ♀ x Purps x Space Queen ♂

 50-100 g/plant in; 750 g/plant out

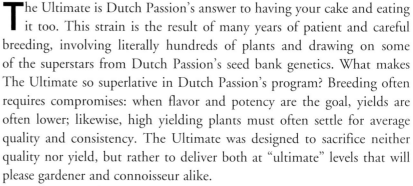

The Ultimate
Dutch Passion

 50/50

 potent, stoney, relaxing

 rich citrus haze

 56–70 days

 undisclosed indica and sativa

 550g per m2 in 400–500g per plant out

 in/greenhouse preferred

The Ultimate is Dutch Passion's answer to having your cake and eating it too. This strain is the result of many years of patient and careful breeding, involving literally hundreds of plants and drawing on some of the superstars from Dutch Passion's seed bank genetics. What makes The Ultimate so superlative in Dutch Passion's program? Breeding often requires compromises: when flavor and potency are the goal, yields are often lower; likewise, high yielding plants must often settle for average quality and consistency. The Ultimate was designed to sacrifice neither quality nor yield, but rather to deliver both at "ultimate" levels that will please gardener and connoisseur alike.

Combining indica and sativa genetics to create a high quality 50/50 offspring is more difficult than many would expect. The challenge is to fully stabilize characteristics such as height, yield, and the consistency of the stone. Beyond its even balance of indica and sativa, the details of The Ultimate's genetic heritage remain a closely guarded Dutch Passion secret.

The Ultimate grows into a dense stout and resilient plant, reaching average heights of 2–2.5 feet (60–75 cm) at finish. The short stature is ideally suited to the indoor grower who wants big yields of top-drawer stash but has space limitations. This plant's uniform growth habits lead to an even canopy in the grow room or greenhouse, which helps to maximize light exposure. Moderate to strong nutrients are recommended during the vegetative phase to help beef up stem sturdiness. This pine-tree shaped plant is best grown with multiple branches, which should be supported due to the stem-breaking heft of its buds. The Ultimate's hybrid foliage is neither fat nor thin, and may gain red or blue hues as the plants finish. Inexperienced growers should not get too impatient because there is an exceptional growth spurt during the last two weeks of flowering that pumps up the yield. These sticky crystal-covered plants exude a strong sweet aroma that may require stealth measures. While it can make nice finger hash, accidental brushing against plants leaves a strong odor on clothes for hours afterwards.

The Ultimate delivers a stone of the highest order. Delicious hints of orange citrus shine through. The flavor sensation is almost tropical and very rich, and the experienced smoker may detect a touch of haze flavors. The high is a heavy-hitter that is best served when relaxing, rather than when activities are on the menu. Friends may want to caution the occasional toker about this strain's high potency before they inhale. Growers and seasoned smokers are likely to find that this strain lives up to its name in terms of its sizeable stash and its connoisseur smoke.

The Story Behind the Ultimate

Dutch Passion breeders pride themselves on having exacting standards. They seek out high-quality genetics and then look for outstanding individual plants among the hundreds that are grown out. The selected individuals serve as the basis for Dutch Passion's breeding program, so they must possess the qualities that lead to superb varieties. A lot of discernment goes into every Dutch Passion selection. So when breeders were visibly excited over the variety that became "The Ultimate," everyone was curious to find out why. It was a good sign that this variety had bountiful yields worthy of enthusiasm. But the true test would be in the "blind" testing trials.

Testing trials are "blind" tests because the smoker does not know the identity of the strain they receive. This is to ensure that their assessments are not biased by associating the variety name with their experience. This allows new strains to be compared against known, "standard" strains. It's a tough job, but someone has to do it! In this instance, Dutch Passion calls on the expertise of some highly experienced Dutch smoke-testers who are skilled in discerning the good from the outstanding.

When the smoke testers got hold of this strain, they were just as passionate as the breeders had been, declaring that the potency and excellent taste were top-shelf. Ever cautious and skeptical, the strain was evaluated again without any other strains that might influence the assessment. Again, the testers were adamant: this was a special strain. Several of them started calling it "the ultimate" variety, and the name stuck.

Time and time again in controlled smoke trials, The Ultimate has been voted most potent. It is this feedback that has convinced Dutch Passion that the variety deserves its name. In terms of yield, this plant is in the top 10% of what can be achieved. This yield potential combined with the high quality stash has convinced Dutch Passion that The Ultimate is "quite possibly the most important strain our breeders have ever created."

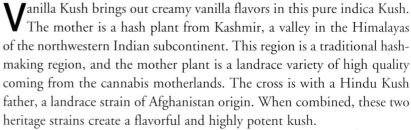

Vanilla Kush

Barney's Farm

I

relaxed, trippy

vanilla musk

60–65 days

♀Kashmir x
♂Afghani

40g per plant in
100–200g per plant
out

Vanilla Kush brings out creamy vanilla flavors in this pure indica Kush. The mother is a hash plant from Kashmir, a valley in the Himalayas of the northwestern Indian subcontinent. This region is a traditional hash-making region, and the mother plant is a landrace variety of high quality coming from the cannabis motherlands. The cross is with a Hindu Kush father, a landrace strain of Afghanistan origin. When combined, these two heritage strains create a flavorful and highly potent kush.

Landrace kush strains are consistent plants with a strong, steady growth pattern. Vanilla Kush likes to branch and typically forms eight symmetrical side branches. This variety delivers happier, more abundant yields when cultivated as multi-branch plants. The solid growth adapts well to hydro and soil systems, and thrives when a SCROG setup is used. When grown indoors, plants typically finish at a height of around 2 feet (60cm) and take roughly 9 weeks to flower. Outdoors, these plants finish at the end of September. With two months' flowering time, outdoor plants can yield up to 8 ounces (250g) apiece.

Vanilla Kush is an iconic, medium-dark plant that stays green throughout and only fades in color as the buds finish. The leaves have thick velvety leaflets with a heavy sugar coating of trichomes hugging close to the leaf base. The glands darken into little globules of red and gold as the plant reaches maturity, and the hairs take on a bright burnished orange hue. Kushes are known to form large, sturdy, and dense colas, and Vanilla Kush is no different. It is notably distinct due to its intensely rich aromas, mixing herbal smells of lavender with the deeper tones of vanilla bean and some acrid accents of citrus peel.

Vanilla Kush placed second in the 2009 overall Cannabis Cup, an accolade that speaks to its appealing combination of creamy flavors and potent effect. Kushes are known for their high THC levels, and this variety delivers a potent and long lasting high that is particularly strong in its physical effects. Vanilla Kush is also a standout on taste. The strong, sweet herbal-floral notes dominate the smoke. This variety induces a strong sense of relaxation, easing muscle tension, which appeals to many medical marijuana users. In smaller amounts, the mental effect is euphoric and thoughtful, yet relaxed. Heavy indulgence strengthens the effects, leading to a trippy and potentially sleepy tunnel vision that may cause couchlock or napping.

Vortex

TGAgenetics Subcool Seeds

Welcome to the vortex, a mental house of mirrors in the marijuana kingdom. This mind-bending cross was bred by Subcool from his favorite old and new headstash. The mother is the Apollo 13 and the father is a Space Queen. After testing many hybrids of these strains, the pungent sour-sweet Vortex hybrid was selected. It is a heavily resinous bubble hash strain with a potent, racing high that leans heavily on the more psychedelic spectrum of the cannabis realm.

When left untopped, Vortex forms the classic tree shape, but plants deliver the best yields when topped early and trained to form multiple growing heads. This variety wilts noticeably during the dark period, almost appearing to need watering. Gardeners should remove heavy low side branches to focus the plant's energy on its uppermost shoots. When plants are topped and placed into flowering at 3 feet (1 meter), they finish well under 5 feet (1.75 meters) but will be very wide. This plant is ideal for a SCROG garden.

 80/20

 speedy, mindbending

 pineapple and peach baby food

 56 days

 ♀Apollo 13 x ♂Space Queen

 150g per plant

 in preferred

Using these methods can deliver an average of 5 ounces (150g) per plant in soil, and more in hydro systems. Subcool prefers organic nutrients to arrive at the best taste and cleanest ash.

Outdoors, Vortex matures more quickly than the typical sativa, resisting late season mildew. Good reports have been reported for many different types of gardening environments from various parts of the world, so long as the grow season allows the plant to flower for a full 8 weeks. Lots of stakes and string are recommended, since the outdoor Vortex plant grows into a wide sagging bush with hundreds of bud sites that benefit from support.

These plants become bright green with vivid red pistils that fade to a more muted rusty brown as the flowers ripen. The many triangle-shaped, hard and dense buds give the plant a redbud look. The leaves definitely lean toward the sativa, growing blade-thin with a coating of small raised trichomes. Vortex clones easily, but is also very uniform when grown from seeds, with almost no phenotypic variation. The females are nearly identical in smell, taste, and growth characteristics.

The Vortex buzz can be energizing and heart racing, but it can also be ripped under, curled under stupid stoned. This high has virtually no ceiling, so that the high keeps climbing without a burnout point. When used lightly, this strain is a real pick-up for the senses, stoking creative juices and provoking thought. With heavier use, Vortex becomes mentally confusing and potentially disorienting.

Even veterans can find themselves spinning and swirling in the vortex of its psychedelic influences.

This strain may take discipline due to its sweet-tart aromas and flavors that leave one's lips smacking for another taste. Some have compared the smell to a mango drink with tart lemonade overtones. The flavor has a similar mix of smooth fruit flavors, likened to peach baby food, mixed with a sweet astringency reminiscent of pineapple. Vortex is definitely dizzying headstash of the highest rank, and has also gained a following from those who use marijuana medically for chronic pain because it assuages physical pain but also calms many of the emotions that accompany the experience of chronic pain.

1st place, 2010 *High Times* Medicinal Cup, San Francisco

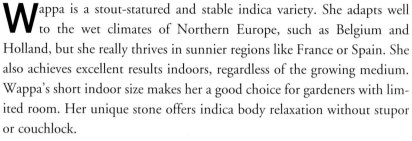

Wappa

Paradise Seeds

 100% indica

 energtic

 pungent fruit, marshmallows

 55-60 days

 indicas

 400-500 g/m² in; 400-500/plant out

 SOG

Wappa is a stout-statured and stable indica variety. She adapts well to the wet climates of Northern Europe, such as Belgium and Holland, but she really thrives in sunnier regions like France or Spain. She also achieves excellent results indoors, regardless of the growing medium. Wappa's short indoor size makes her a good choice for gardeners with limited room. Her unique stone offers indica body relaxation without stupor or couchlock.

Wappa is a feminized variety: pollen was obtained from a female manipulated to produce male flowers, so all of Wappa's seeds will produce females. She is a robust plant that quickly becomes the darling of the grow room because of her attractive appearance, ease in cultivation and fast ripening and yield. Her broad leaves shine with lime-green healthiness. She starts a bit slowly, but soon gets her pace, turning into a picture-perfect little spruce with one main stem. When forced to flower at 1 foot (30 cm), she doubles in size by maturity, producing big chunky colas that fill the air with sweet aromas of fruits and sugar. Wappa has a high calyx-to-leaf ratio, which makes her a breeze to manicure. She finishes flowering in about 8 weeks, by which time her buds and the neighboring leaves will be coated in resin that smells like marshmallows. This variety produces about half a kilogram (about 1 pound) of buds per square meter indoors, or roughly the same amount per plant, outdoors.

Wappa's fruity nugs are great head candy. Her THC has been measured at over 18% on all samples, making for an intense high. The buzz comes on strong, but with a pleasant rather than jarring onset. It is a luminous high that nudges open the doors of perception. After a few hours, the heightened awareness fades off slowly, leaving an appreciation for the mini-vacation that Wappa has created. Even though she is a full indica, Wappa does not weigh down the body or create couchlock for most people. She taps into an active, aware body vibe, more conducive to merrymaking than couch surfing.

White Berry
Paradise Seeds

IS 75/25

happy, lucid

berry, lemon

45-50 days/early Oct.

indica ♀ x indica/
sativa hybrid reversed
female plant ♂

400-500 g/m²

SOG

White Berry is a happy-go-lucky plant that is very fast to flower and particularly well suited to sea of green grows. Because her seeds have been feminized, White Berry plants are all-female, with no sexing required. When this variety was tested, none of her seeds showed hermaphrodite tendencies—there was not a single male flower formation among these ladies.

White Berry is model marijuana, slender and medium in height, with fresh green good looks and a single-cola dominance and homogeneity between the plants that will endear her to sea of green gardeners. These plants come up in a uniform pattern that makes growing and budding as easy as growing from clones. The White Berry calyx-to-leaf ratio is good news for weed manicurists, because she is easy to trim. Her smaller leaves are also worth recycling for excellent hashish.

In her short 7-week flowering phase, White Berry becomes bejeweled with trichomes that frost her buds, and she generates a decidedly berry perfume that leaves no doubt about the appropiateness of her name. Some calyxes may turn purple, giving them an exotic and mouthwatering appearance. Although the buds will look as if they are on the verge of ripeness at 6 weeks, it is best to leave them another 10 days to allow the cannabinoids to reach their peak. By then, the ripened buds will add a fresh astringent lemon to the unmistakable berry scent, like a mixture of berry jam and citrus. The flowers will have bulked out, achieving yields in the 400-500 grams per square meter range.

White Berry's hybridized genetics create a complex and versatile smoke. The typical result is a crystalline sativa head high, complementary to most lightweight activities. Yet when smoked in higher quantities, an indica-style body stone comes forward, like a warmth radiating over the smoker's torso and limbs. Tokers who smoke lightly throughout the day, but want a deeper stone at night, may find that White Berry meets all their needs in one attractive, easy-growing package.

White Rhino
Green House Seed Company

Photo: Jan Otsen

White Rhino is a strong, fast-growing, near-pure indica with ancestry in the same lineage as her more famous relative, White Widow. As the name suggests, this plant is tough and sturdy, with a thick skin for high temperatures as well as cold nights. This strain delivers a knockout, medicinal-grade indica stone.

White Rhino adapts well to any environment, and is known for her massive yields, especially in hydro grows. Green House recommends starting her with a medium-low pH (5.7 hydro, 5.8 soil) that is slowly increased until it reaches 6.5 at the end of flowering. EC levels should be kept under 2.4 in hydro and 2.0 in soil. Plants ripen in 9 weeks, or early October. To really see the rhino's "white," let her ripen one extra week.

While these plants flourish in SOG or SCROG systems, they can also be grown in larger containers and allowed to vegetate into bushes. The White Rhino plant has a typical short squat stature, with short, thick branches and extremely compact internodes. She is a smart choice for indoor gardeners with space limitations, or outdoor growers looking for a shorter plant. Plants grown in 5-gallon containers will finish at 4-5 feet (1.2-1.5m) if allowed to grow vegetatively for at least two weeks. With less veg time, or in small containers, plants stay at about 3 feet (1 m) tall. Even plants with no root limitations finish no taller than 6 feet (2m). When White Rhino is allowed to grow big, pruning is necessary to allow light and air to penetrate the inner and lower areas of the plant.

The leaves on White Rhino are huge, full, and midnight green, and her stalks are very thick. Her calyxes are small, round and super dense, forming rock hard colas. While not terribly odiferous while growing, the White Rhino harvest will have a pleasantly sweet smell. The toke is also sweetened with indica berry flavor, followed by a sharp aftertaste and sometimes a bout of coughing. White Rhino delivers a full-throttle indica stone. The buzz goes straight to the body, giving a rubbery, relaxed feeling that is nearly narcotic. It is a down-tempo smoke that endures, ideal for slow-paced recreation. White Rhino is prized in the medical community for effective relief of chronic pain.

2nd Prize, *High Times* Cannabis Cup 1996, Bio category
2nd Prize Champions Cup, Madrid 2005

 90/10

 relaxing, physical, narcotic

 sweet, acrid aftertaste

 63 days/early Oct.

 Afghan ♀ x Brazilian/ South Indian ♂

 500-600g/m² in; up to 1200g/plant out

 SOG

White Russian
Serious Seeds

White Russian combines AK-47 with the White Widow to produce a snowy plant with a pleasantly sweet aroma and a strong, clear high. It was not until much later that Serious Seeds breeder, Simon, became aware of the alcoholic cocktail by the same name.

This easy-to-grow plant works equally well in soil or hydro. Intermediate in size, White Russian is not very leafy, giving it an open canopy that makes it perfect for indoor gardening. This plant is appropriate for a sea of green method. The yield is excellent, with a normal harvest producing 350-450 grams per square meter.

The mottled green colas resemble their indica heritage in size and density, and are typically coated with light tan crystals. At maturity, the hairs turn to auburn. White Russian buds smell sweet and green, with a light undertone of skunk. The sweetness is enhanced in the flavor, although heavier like hash oil rather than lighter like flowers.

An expansive smoke, White Russian has a clear high with long duration. The effect can be complex, but tends toward wakefulness rather than sleep, and may have some trippy or spacey dimensions: A good afternoon smoke with a cup of coffee when you're ready to kick back and relax.

Overall Winner *High Times* Cannabis Cup 1997
Winner High Times Cannabis Cup,
Organic Pot 1996

 alert, clear

 sweet, pungent

 58-62 days

 White Widow x AK-47

 350-450 g per m²

White Satin
Mandala Seeds

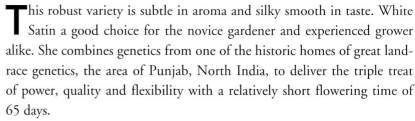

This robust variety is subtle in aroma and silky smooth in taste. White Satin a good choice for the novice gardener and experienced grower alike. She combines genetics from one of the historic homes of great landrace genetics, the area of Punjab, North India, to deliver the triple treat of power, quality and flexibility with a relatively short flowering time of 65 days.

White Satin has a slim growth pattern, with medium-long side shoots and a generous main bud that is perfect for sea of green from seed or clone. This 50/50 hybrid is also versatile enough to make a good SCROG or multi-branch plant. White Satin's main flower power is located on her central stem, but her side shoots also deliver quality "nuggets." The stems are firm and can easily support heavy colas in outdoor locations. Even under low light, such as under fluorescent tubes, White Satin's performance is very satisfying; however, for optimal yields, Mandala recommends 400 watts or more per square meter. White Satin also performs well when grown in soil with organic nutrients. This strain's medium height, good yield and well-balanced, intensive high have made her a popular variety for all levels of indoor cultivators. Plants can be started and harvested with fairly minimal effort.

Because White Satin can develop an extremely large and dense main cola, during the last 2 weeks of flowering it's a good idea to keep humidity under 50%, and temperature above 68°F (20°C) in the dark cycle, as a preventative measure against mold. Outdoors, she does best up to 48 degrees latitude or in climates with a dry autumn.

White Satin's buds are characterized by a broad oval shape and large calyxes. The most resinous plants will cover many leaves with trichomes and provide an extra treat for hash enthusiasts. White Satin's growing odor is light—and stealthy—but pleasant. The cured buds exude a mild apricot aroma and a fresh sweet taste. This is a pleasure smoke, with a fresh, mentally stimulating high, but no heavy body or mind incapacitation. That makes her a great, functional choice for a daytime enjoyment.

 50/50

 clear, uplifting

 mellow apricot

 65 days

 landrace genetics from Punjab, North India

 400-500g/m² under 400w/m2

 SOG

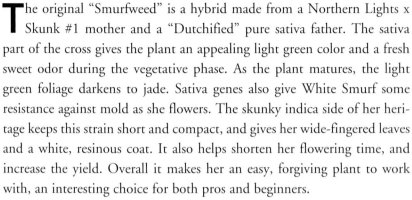

White Smurf
Ceres Seeds

T he original "Smurfweed" is a hybrid made from a Northern Lights x Skunk #1 mother and a "Dutchified" pure sativa father. The sativa part of the cross gives the plant an appealing light green color and a fresh sweet odor during the vegetative phase. As the plant matures, the light green foliage darkens to jade. Sativa genes also give White Smurf some resistance against mold as she flowers. The skunky indica side of her heritage keeps this strain short and compact, and gives her wide-fingered leaves and a white, resinous coat. It also helps shorten her flowering time, and increase the yield. Overall it makes her an easy, forgiving plant to work with, an interesting choice for both pros and beginners.

White Smurf can be grown indoors, in a greenhouse, or outdoors depending on the climate. Indoors, White Smurf grows to medium height, with a solid bud and not many side-branches. With a little pruning at the start of flowering, White Smurf is very suitable for the sea of green method. This plant develops beautiful solid, sticky, snow-dusted colas. Little towers of calyxes sprout on her buds when she flowers. As the buds become covered with crystals, the flowers themselves remain green and white with orange accents in their hairs, a trait marking the skunk side of the hybrid.

Reflecting her skunk and sativa heritage, White Smurf's flavor has been described as "full and rich," "musky-but-sweet" and "powerful," but it has also been described as "fresh" and "citrus-like." Her stone is both relaxing and wakeful. After one joint, this strain gives a deep, warm body-buzz that feels like walking through water, but doesn't stupefy or lead to snores. White Smurf starts a smooth reggae rhythm pulsing though your body, a social, happy, positive vibe that makes a superb after-dinner smoke. Cannabis Cup attendees agreed – they showed their appreciation by awarding this strain with the People's Choice as well as the overall Cup in 2000.

 50/50

 body warming

 citrus and musk

 45-55 days in/ Oct. out

 hybrid ♀ (Northern Lights x Skunk #1) x pure sativa ♂

 0.85 g/watt of light in; 350 g/plant out

 greenhouse

 SOG

White Widow
Green House Seed Co.

Since its introduction in 1995, White Widow has become an infamous breed in the world of weed. This variety can be found in almost every coffeeshop in Amsterdam, but while imitation may be the truest form of flattery, the genuine item bears the Greenhouse name.

This variety's reputation has been built on its excellence in smell, flavor, and quality of the high. White Widow has fragrantly fresh pine cone nugs that have a taste bordering between fruit and flowers when smoked. Setting the standard for kind bud, White Widow washes over you with a warm feeling of impending stoniness. While the buzz is strong, it is not sedating, producing a mixture of effects that are both cerebral and physical, but may include both spacy or mildly trippy sensations.

White Widow is a compact plant of medium height. The buds only develop a few amber-colored hairs, but the outrageous crystalline resin production of this plant has become legendary. Inevitably the reputation that precedes it leads some growers to decide that it is overrated, but many find this variety to be everything they anticipated and more. White Widow has the potential to live up to its reputation when grown adeptly. This strain is recommended for indoor gardening, where water and fertilizer should be administered modestly to avoid mildew and retain the delicious flavors. Greenhouse suggests changing the lighting to 8 hours during the last 2 weeks of flowering in order to halt regrowth on the buds and produce just enough stress to coax out the maximum amount of sticky resin per inch.

1st place, *High Times* Cannabis Cup bio category 1995

 60/40

 giggly, blissful

 caramel, coffee, earthy

 56-63 days/late Oct.

 Mendo "Purps" clone only ♀ x Purps x Space Queen ♂

 50-100 g/plant in; 750 g/plant out

 SOG

A-Train • Afghanica • AK 47 • American Dream
Lights • Aurora B. • Barney's Farm Blue chees
God Bud • BC Sweet Tooth • Big Bang • Big B
Cheese • Blueberry • Bubble Cheese • Buddh
Chronic • Double Dutch • Dr. Grinspoon • Dutch
Super Bud • First Lady • Flo • Fruit of the Gods
• Hashberry • Hawaiian Snow • Headband • I
Jack the Ripper • Jacky White • Jilly Bean • K
• Léda Uno • Lemon Skunk • Lowryder #2 • L
• Mazar • Medicine Man • Morning Glory • Mo
Diesel • Northern Lights • Northern Lights-H
Power Plant • Querkle • Sage • Skunk Haze
• Super Lemon Haze • Super Silver Haze • Ta
The Pure Skunk #I • The Purps • The Ultima
• White Rhino • White Russian • Wh

Amnesia Haze • Arctic Sun •Atomic Northern
• Barney's Farm GI3 Haze • BC Blueberry • BC
d • Big Buddha Cheese • Black Domina • Blue
Haze • California Indica • Cheesus • Chiesel •
en's Royal Orange • Easy Rider • Ed Rosenthal
ruity Thai • G Bomb • Grape Kush • Hash Plant
• Iranian Autoflower • Jack F6 • Jack Herer •
Mist • Kalichakra • Kushage • LA Confidential
• Mango • Master Kush • Matanuska Tundra
ation • Nebula • Nevil's Haze • New York City
e • NYPD • Orange Bud • Pineapple Punch •
rawberry Cough • Strawberry Haze (Arjan's)
e Gold • The Church • The Doctor • The Kali
Vanilla Kush • Vortex • Wappa • White Berry
Satin • White Smurf • White Widow

Appendixes

Glossary

aeroponics: growing plants by misting roots that are suspended in air

apical tip: the growing tip of the plant

backcrossing: crossing of an offspring with one of the parents to reinforce a trait

bract: small reduced leaflet in cannabis that appears below a pair of calyxes

calyx: pod harboring the female ovule and two pistils, seed pod

CBC: cannabichromene—one of several non-psychoactive cannabinoids

CBD: cannabidiol—one of several non-psycho-active cannabinoids; it is anti-inflammatory

F1 generation: first filial generation, the off-spring of two parent (P1) plants

F2 generation: second filial generation, the off-spring of two F1 plants

feminized: a seed that will produce only 100% female plants

hydroponics: growing plants in nutrient solution without soil

indica: plant originating in the 30th parallel typified by wide, dark green or purple vegetation; it grows short internodes with profuse branching that forms a wide pyramid shape usually no more than 6 feet tall

internodes: the space between nodes

node: a section of the stem where leaves and side shoots arise; nodes are often swollen, and are sometimes referred to as joints

P1: first parental generation, the parents crossed to form F1 or F1 hybrid offspring

pistils (stigmas): small pair of fuzzy white hairs extending from top of the calyx, designed to capture pollen floating in the air

pollen: the male reproductive product that fertilizes the female flower, a cream-colored or yellow dust released by the male flower which floats along air currents to reach the female

psychoactive: affecting the consciousness or psyche

ruderalis: plant originating from the 50–55th parallel in Russia, typified by the auto flowering of the plant based on age instead of lighting schemes

sativa: plant originating from the 45–50th parallel typified by a tall pine-tree-like growth habit (5 to 15 feet), long internodes, light green color and airy buds

screen of green (SCROG): A technique for supporting plants; a net is secured to a frame and held horizontally so the branches grow through the holes; the nets hold the branches in place so they don't bend or droop and helps support them when they are heavily laden with buds

sea of green (SOG): indoor method for growing marijuana in which many plants are grown close together with little time spent in vegetative growth; rather than a few plants growing large and filling the canopy, many smaller plants are forced into flowering creating a lower canopy and earlier harvest

sepal: a modified leaf located at the base of a flower

stipule: the section where the plant stem meets the leaf stem, or petiole

strain: a line of offspring derived from common ancestors

terpene: class of chemicals composed of repeating units of isoprene (C5H8) to form chains or 3D structures; associated with various scents and may be responsible for the varied highs in cannabis

THC: tetrahydrocannabinol, primary psychoactive component of cannabis

trichome: plant hair that is either glandular (secreting) or eglandular (non secreting)

wpf: watts per square foot

wpm: watts per square meter

When Will Your Outdoor Plants Mature?

Cannabis flowers based on the number of hours of uninterrupted dark period it receives. When a critical period is reached for several days the plant changes its growth from vegetative to flowering. During the spring and summer the number of hours of darkness shrinks as the latitude increases. For instance, on June 16, close to June 22, the longest day of the year and the first day of summer, there are 9½ hours of darkness at the 35th latitude, near Memphis, Albuquerque and Los Angeles. At the 40th parallel, close to New York, Columbus and Denver the dark period is 9 hours, a difference of half an hour. However, the seed producer's latitudes are considerably different than the latitudes of the gardens of many outdoor growers. Vancouver, at the 50th parallel and Holland at the 52nd parallel have 7:49 and 7:27 hours of darkness respectively on that date. As a result, maturity dates change significantly with changes in latitude.

To find the ripening date at your latitude:

1. Count back from the outdoor ripening date the number of days the variety takes to flower indoors. This is the trigger date, the date that the plant changes from vegetative to flowering phase.
2. Locate the breeder's latitude at the trigger date. The chart (next page) indicates the number of hours of darkness that trigger the plant to flower.
3. On the column representing your latitude, locate the date on the chart that matches the dark period from #2.
4. Count forward the number of days it takes to ripen indoors. The result is the maturity date.

Figuring Ripening Dates: Examples

A variety from Holland ripens there on October 15 and matures in 70 days indoors. Counting back on the latitude chart you see that on August 1, about 75 days before ripening, the plant triggered on 8½ hours of darkness. Along the 40th parallel or further south, the dark period never gets below 9 hours of darkness. The variety will be triggered to flower almost as soon as it is placed outside. If it's planted outdoors June 1 it will ripen in 70 days, near August 10. If planted June 16 it will ripen in late August. At the 45th parallel, the plant will be triggered to flower around July 1. The buds will mature September 10–15.

A Canadian variety adapted to the 50th parallel ripens October 16 outdoors, 60 days after forcing indoors. Counting back to Aug 16, 60 days before the bud matures, the dark period at the 50th parallel is about 9 ½ hours. At the 45th parallel this dark period occurs August 4, with a ripening date of around October 4. At the 40th parallel it occurs around July 30, with a harvest around September 30. At the 35th parallel and lower latitudes, flowering is triggered as soon as the plants are planted since there are only a few days around June 22 when the dark period stretches longer than 9½ hours. If planted June 1, the plants will ripen in early August.

NUMBER OF HOURS OF DARKNESS BY LATITUDE

Latitude	0	+10	+20	+30	+35	+40	+45	+50	+52	+54	+56	+58
June 16	11:53	11:18	10:40	9:56	9:30	8:59	8:24	7:49	7:27	6:53	6:25	5:53
July 1	11:53	11:18	10:41	9:57	9:31	9:01	8:26	7:41	7:21	6:57	6:29	5:55
July 16	11:53	11:21	10:46	10:08	9:44	9:17	8:45	8:05	7:47	7:25	7:01	7:33
Aug. 1	11:53	11:27	10:59	10:26	10:06	9:44	9:19	8:48	8:32	8:15	7:57	7:35
Aug. 16	11:53	11:34	11:13	10:48	10:33	10:17	9:58	9:35	9:27	9:12	9:59	9:43
Sept. 1	11:53	11:42	11:29	11:15	11:06	10:57	10:45	10:29	10:25	10:18	10:10	10:02
Sept. 16	11:53	11:50	11:46	11:41	11:39	11:35	11:31	11:27	11:24	11:22	11:21	11:16
Oct. 1	11:53	11:59	12:03	12:08	12:11	12:14	12:18	12:22	12:24	12:26	12:28	12:30
Oct. 16	11:53	12:07	12:19	12:35	12:43	12:53	13:06	13:17	13:23	13:30	13:36	13:45
Nov. 1	11:53	12:13	12:36	13:01	13:15	13:31	13:49	14:14	14:24	14:35	14:48	15:03
Nov. 16	11:53	12:21	12:50	13:22	13:42	14:03	14:29	15:00	15:14	15:30	15:49	16:09
Dec. 1	11:53	12:26	13:00	13:39	14:03	14:27	14:58	15:36	16:07	16:14	16:36	17:02
Dec. 16	11:53	12:27	13:05	13:56	14:12	14:40	15:12	15:54	16:13	16:36	17:01	17:31

Garden Size: Lighting & Yield

Size	Area	Watts	Lamp Choices	Yield (grams)
1 sq ft (0.09 sq m)	1' x 1' (0.3 x 0.3 m)	40–80w	CFLs with bowl reflectors/circular or u-tube fluorescent bulbs	10–80g
4 sq ft (0.36 sq m)	2' x 2' (0.6 x 0.6 m)	200–240w	HID (MH or HPS) T5 Fluorescents	50–250g
8 sq ft (0.75 sq m)	4' x 2' (1.25 x 0.6 m)	350–480w	T5 Fluorescents, smaller HIDs, or large HIDs on a track light shuttle	90–480g
9 sq ft (0.8 sq m)	3' x 3' (0.9 x 0.9 m)	400–600w	HPS or MH	100–600g
16 sq ft (1.55 sq m)	4' x 4' (1.25 x 1.25 m)	600–1000w	HPS or MH	300–1000g
25 sq ft (2.3 sq m)	5' x 5' (1.5 x 1.5 m)	2 x 750w (1500w)	HPS or MH	400–750g
32 sq ft (3 sq m)	4' x 8' (1.25 x 2.45 m)	3 x 600w 2 x 750w 2 x 1000w (1500–2000w)	HPS or MH	700–2000g

Note: CFL is an abbreviation for compact fluorescent lights. HID stands for High Intensity Discharge lights. The two types most commonly used in indoor gardens are MH (Metal Halide) and HPS (High Pressure Sodium).

2008 Daily UV Index

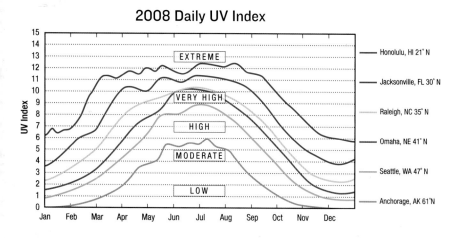

Metric Conversion

Mass

1 gram (g) =	0.035 ounces (1/28 ounce)
1 ounce (oz) =	28.35 grams
1 pound (lb) =	16 ounces
1 kilogram (kg) =	2.2 pounds
1 pound (lb) =	0.45 kilograms

Length

1 foot (ft) =	30.5 centimeters (1/3 meter)
1 meter (m) =	3.28 feet
1 meter (m) =	100 centimeters
1 inch (in) =	2.54 centimeters

Area

1 square meter (sq m) =	10.76 square feet
1 square foot (sq ft) =	0.09 square meters

Yield

1 ounce per square foot =	305 g per square meter
100 grams per square meter =	0.33 ounces per square foot

Temperature

15°C =	59°F
20°C =	68°F
25°C =	72°F
28°C =	82°F
30°C =	86°F
32°C =	89.5°F
35°C =	95° F

To Calculate:

Celsius = (F-32) x 5/9

Fahrenheit = C x 9/5 +32

Concentration

1ppm = 1 mg/L = 0.0001%

Volumes

1 teaspoon (tsp) =	5 milliliters (ml)
1 tablespoon (tbsp) =	15 milliliters (ml)
1 ounce (oz) =	30 milliliters (ml)
1 cup (c) = 8 flow ounces =	236 milliliters (ml)
1 pint (p) = 2 cups =	473 milliliters (ml)
1 quart (qt) = 2 pints =	946 milliliters (ml)
1 gallon (g) = 4 quarts =	3785 milliliters (ml) 3.785 liters (l)

Sponsors

Thanks to all of the businesses,
organizations and individuals
that supported this project.

Big Book of **BUDS** GREATEST HITS

Marijuana Varieties from the World's Best Breeders
Ed Rosenthal

Trusted for over 25 years
Providing Quality Nutrient Products for Soil and Hydroponics

Elements™   SeaBlast™   Bloom Master™   BioRighteous™   Sugar Peak™

BioZeus™   GodSilica™   Sweet & Heavy™   OilyCann™

Charts and more details, visit **earthjuice.com**

CannabisNow

By including only responsible content, we enlighten, educate and entertain. We provide our audience with the information they need to stay on the cutting edge of industry innovations.

Cannabis Now focuses on the most relevant news, political happenings, cannabis legislation, horticultural advancements, social change, economic trends and medical information.

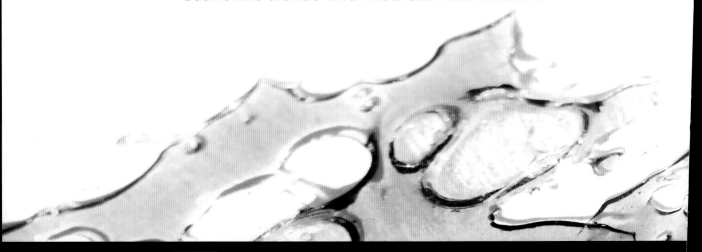

Download Now

the first cannabis magazine accepted by iTunes

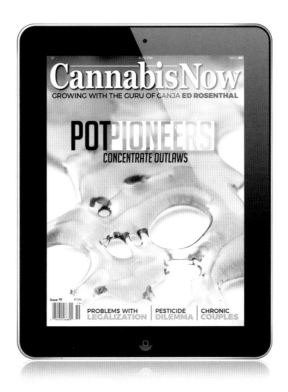

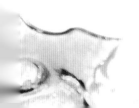

ED KNOWS HOW TO KEEP YOUR PLANTS HEALTHY

Get rid of spider mites and powdery mildew.
Repel pests before they move in.
Eliminate existing infestations.

Natural, environmentally-safe solutions

ED Rosenthal
Grow with the best

www.edrosenthal.com

Strain Journal

Strain name: ....

Date: ....

Smell: ....

Taste: ....

Buzz: ....

Notes: ....

Strain name: ....

Date: ....

Smell: ....

Taste: ....

Buzz: ....

Notes: ....

Strain name: ....

Date: ....

Smell: ....

Taste: ....

Buzz: ....

Notes: ....

Strain name: ....

Date: ....

Smell: ....

Taste: ....

Buzz: ....

Notes: ....

Strain name: ....

Date: ....

Smell: ....

Taste: ....

Buzz: ....

Notes: ....

Strain name: ....

Date: ....

Smell: ....

Taste: ....

Buzz: ....

Notes: ....

Strain name: ....

Date: ....

Smell: ....

Taste: ....

Buzz: ....

Notes: ....

Strain name: ....

Date: ....

Smell: ....

Taste: ....

Buzz: ....

Notes: ....

Strain name: ....

Date: ....

Smell: ....

Taste: ....

Buzz: ....

Notes: ....

Strain name: ....

Date: ....

Smell: ....

Taste: ....

Buzz: ....

Notes: ....

Strain name: ....

Date: ....

Smell: ....

Taste: ....

Buzz: ....

Notes: ....

Strain name: ....

Date: ....

Smell: ....

Taste: ....

Buzz: ....

Notes: ....

Strain name: ....

Date: ....

Smell: ....

Taste: ....

Buzz: ....

Notes: ....

Strain name: ....

Date: ....

Smell: ....

Taste: ....

Buzz: ....

Notes: ....

Strain name: ....

Date: ....

Smell: ....

Taste: ....

Buzz: ....

Notes: ....

Strain name: ....

Date: ....

Smell: ....

Taste: ....

Buzz: ....

Notes: ....

Strain name: ....

Date: ....

Smell: ....

Taste: ....

Buzz: ....

Notes: ....

Strain name: ....

Date: ....

Smell: ....

Taste: ....

Buzz: ....

Notes: ....

Strain name: ....

Date: ....

Smell: ....

Taste: ....

Buzz: ....

Notes: ....

Strain name: ....

Date: ....

Smell: ....

Taste: ....

Buzz: ....

Notes: ....